EASY GUITAR
WITH NOTES & TAB

CHRIS TOMLIN
COLLECTION

2nd EDITION

ISBN 978-1-4950-9317-3

7777 W. BLUEMOUND RD. P.O. BOX 13819 MILWAUKEE, WI 53213

In Australia Contact:
Hal Leonard Australia Pty. Ltd.
4 Lentara Court
Cheltenham, Victoria, 3192 Australia
Email: ausadmin@halleonard.com.au

Visit Hal Leonard Online at
www.halleonard.com

STRUM AND PICK PATTERNS

This chart contains the suggested strum and pick patterns that are referred to by number at the beginning of each song in this book. The symbols ⊓ and ∨ in the strum patterns refer to down and up strokes, respectively. The letters in the pick patterns indicate which right-hand fingers play which strings.

p = thumb
i = index finger
m = middle finger
a = ring finger

For example; Pick Pattern 2
is played: thumb - index - middle - ring

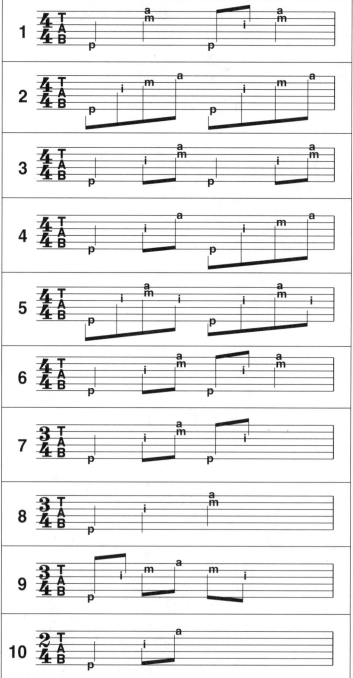

Strum Patterns

Pick Patterns

You can use the 3/4 Strum and Pick Patterns in songs written in compound meter (6/8, 9/8, 12/8, etc.).
For example, you can accompany a song in 6/8 by playing the 3/4 pattern twice in each measure.
The 4/4 Strum and Pick Patterns can be used for songs written in cut time (¢) by doubling the note time values in the patterns. Each pattern would therefore last two measures in cut time.

At the Cross

(Love Ran Red)

Words and Music by Matt Redman, Jonas Myrin, Chris Tomlin, Ed Cash and Matt Armstrong

*Capo I

Strum Pattern: 4
Pick Pattern: 4

Optional: To match recording, place capo at 2nd fret.

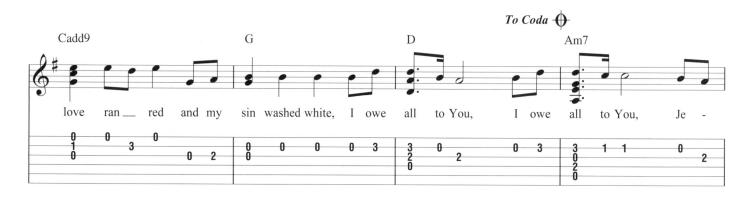

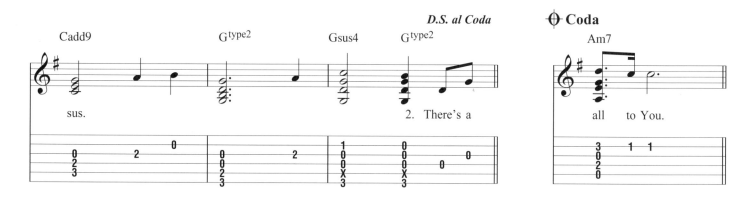

Bridge

Chorus

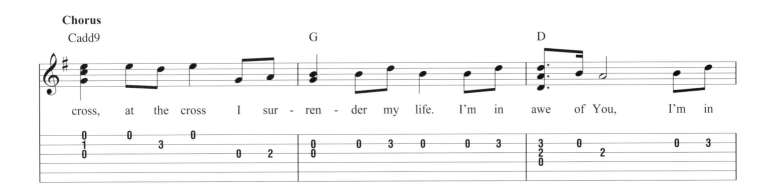

Outro

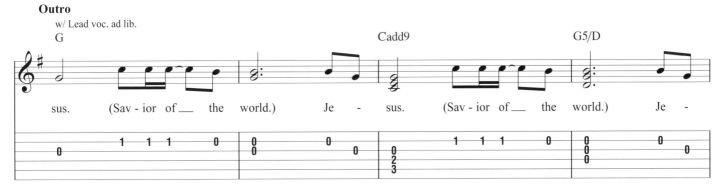

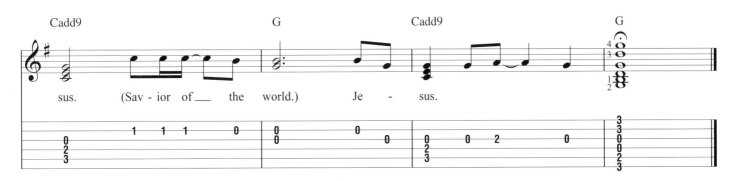

Additional Lyrics

2. There's a place where sin and shame are powerless,
   Where my heart has peace with God and forgiveness,
   Where all the love I've ever found comes like a flood, comes flowing down.

Amazing Grace
(My Chains Are Gone)

Words by John Newton
Traditional American Melody
Additional Words and Music by Chris Tomlin and Louie Giglio

D.S. al Coda 1
(take 2nd ending)

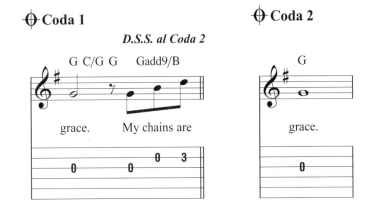

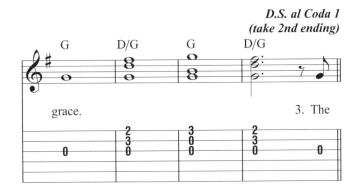

Outro-Verse

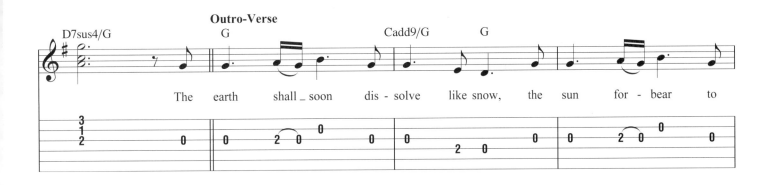

The earth shall _ soon dis - solve like snow, the sun for - bear to

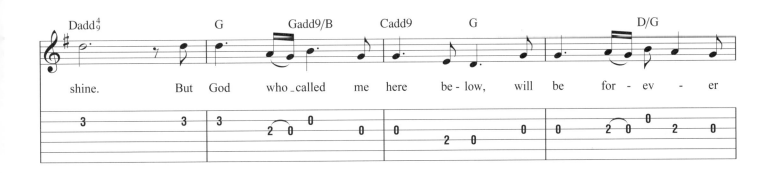

shine. But God who _ called me here be - low, will be for - ev - er

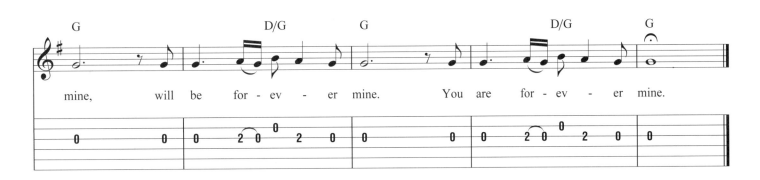

mine, will be for - ev - er mine. You are for - ev - er mine.

Additional Lyrics

2. 'Twas grace that taught my heart to fear,
   And grace my fears relieved.
   How precious did that grace appear
   The hour I first believed.

3. The Lord has promised good to me.
   His word my hope secures.
   He will my shield and portion be,
   As long as life endures.

Forever

Words and Music by Chris Tomlin

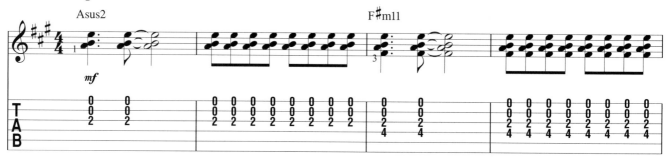

Strum Pattern: 1, 6
Pick Pattern: 4, 6

Intro
Strong Rock beat

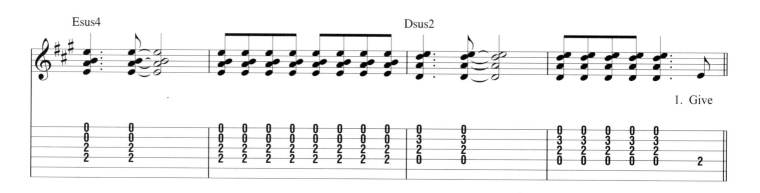

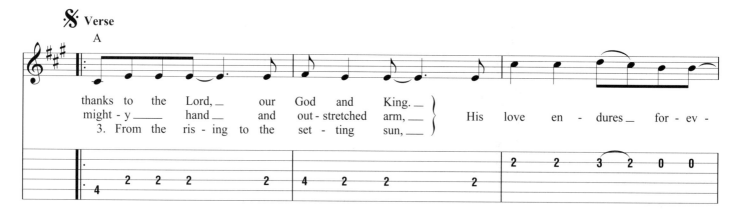

Verse

thanks to the Lord, __ our God and King. __ } His love en - dures __ for - ev -
might - y __ hand __ and out - stretched arm, __ }
3. From the ris - ing to the set - ting sun, __ }

1. Give

- er. ___ { For He is good, __ He is a - bove all things. __ } His
{ For the life ___ that's been re - born, __ }
{ And by the grace of ___ God ___ we will car - ry on. __ }

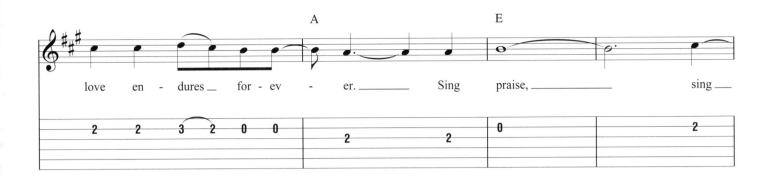

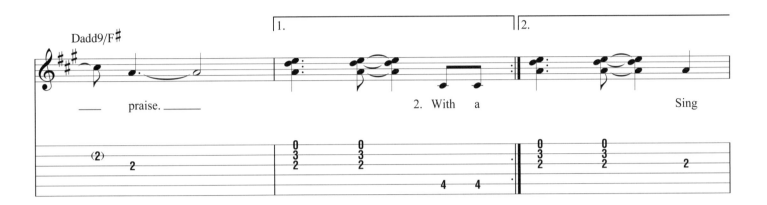

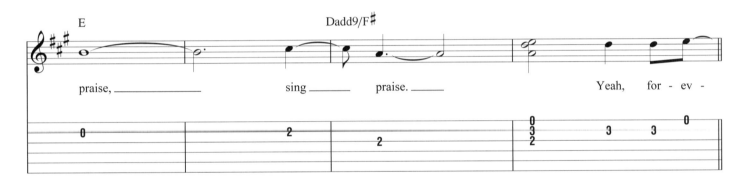

To Coda ⊕

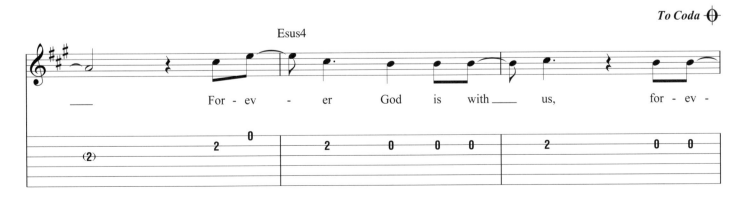

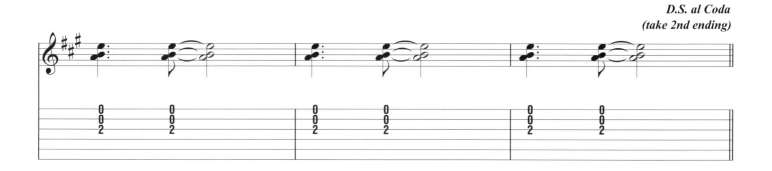

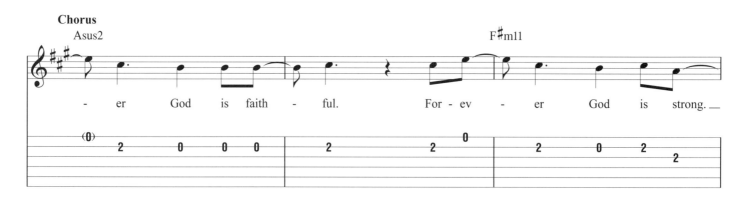

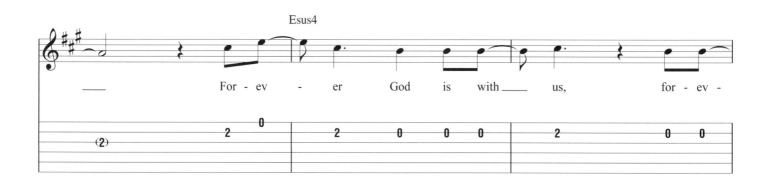

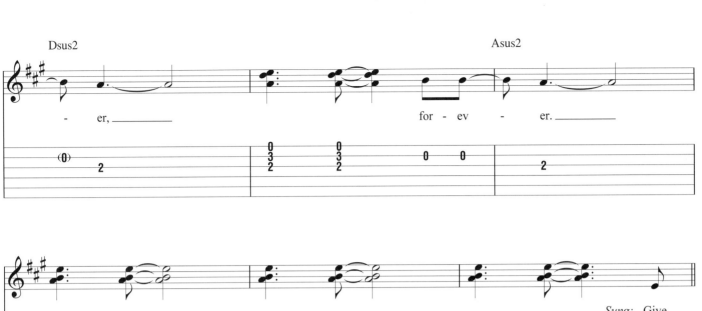

Bridge

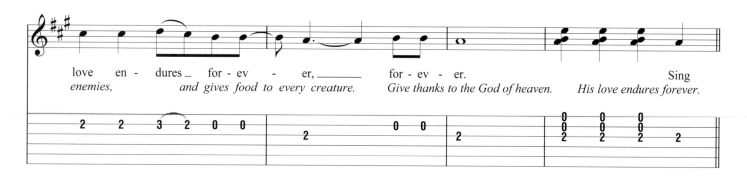

love en- dures for- ev- er, _____ for- ev- er. Sing

enemies, *and gives food to every creature.* *Give thanks to the God of heaven.* *His love endures forever.*

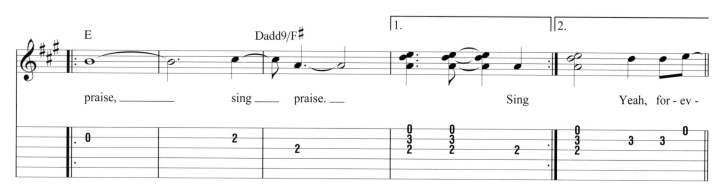

E   Dadd9/F♯ |1. |2.

praise, _____ sing ___ praise. ___   Sing   Yeah, for- ev-

Chorus

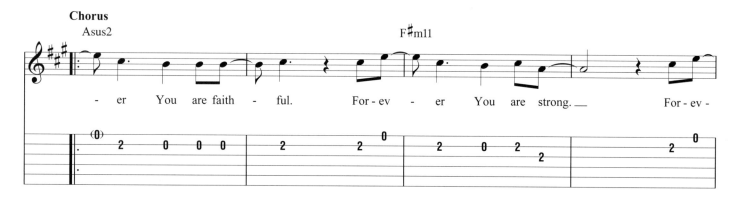

Asus2   F♯m11

- er You are faith - ful. For- ev- er You are strong. ___ For- ev-

Esus4   Dsus2   1., 2.

- er You are with ___ us, for- ev - er. _____ For- ev-

3.

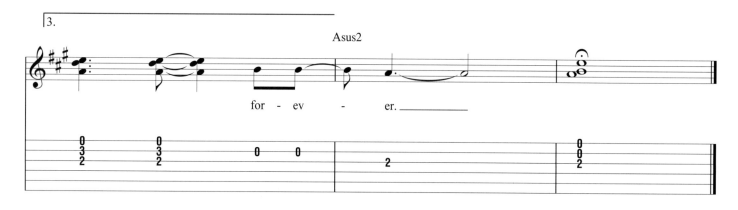

Asus2

for - ev - er. _____

Holy Is the Lord

Words and Music by Chris Tomlin and Louie Giglio

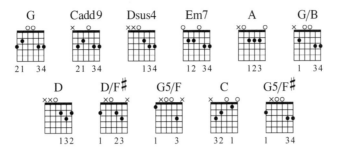

*Capo II

Strum Pattern: 1
Pick Pattern: 3

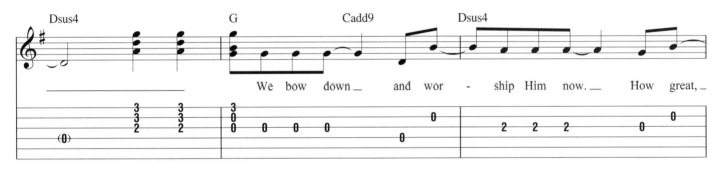

*Optional: To match recording, place capo at 2nd fret.   **Substitute G/B on 2nd verse.

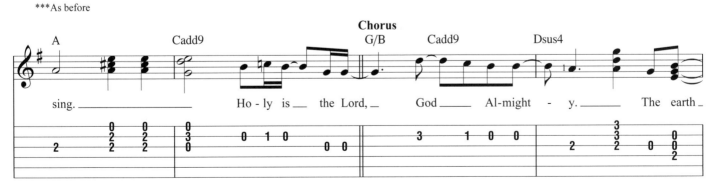

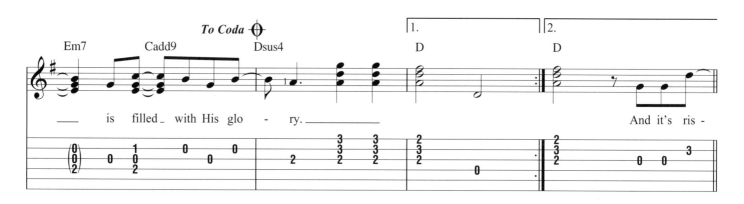

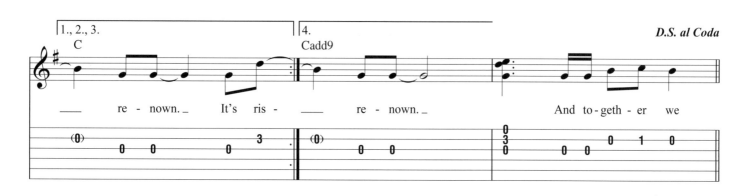

Coda

Interlude

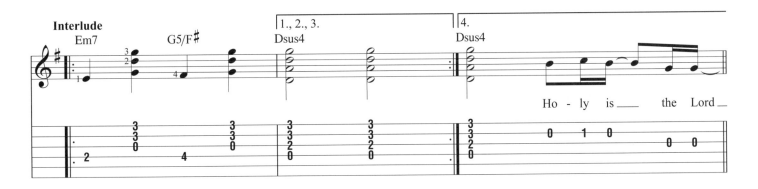

Outro-Chorus

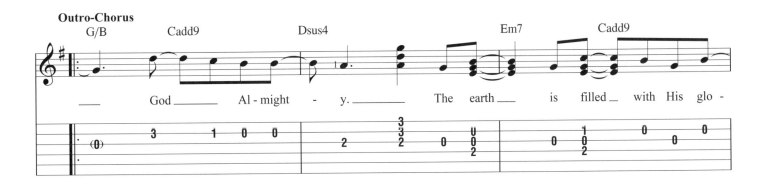

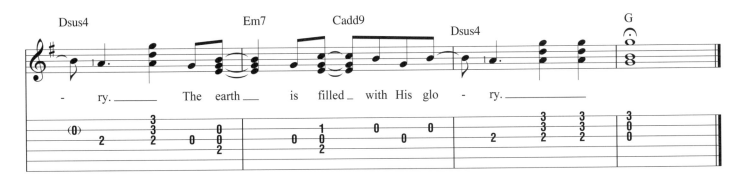

Good Good Father

Words and Music by Pat Barrett and Anthony Brown

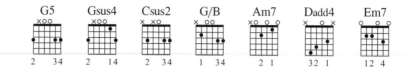

*Capo II

Strum Pattern: 9
Pick Pattern: 7

Verse

Slow, in 2

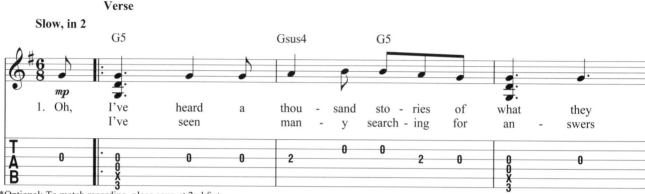

1. Oh, I've heard a thou-sand sto-ries of what they
   I've seen man-y search-ing for an-swers

*Optional: To match recording, place capo at 2nd fret.

think You're like. But I've heard the ten-der whis-per of
far and wide. But I know we're all search-ing for

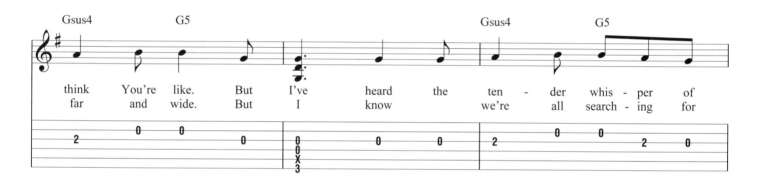

love in the dead of night. And You tell me
an-swers on-ly You pro-vide. 'Cause you know just

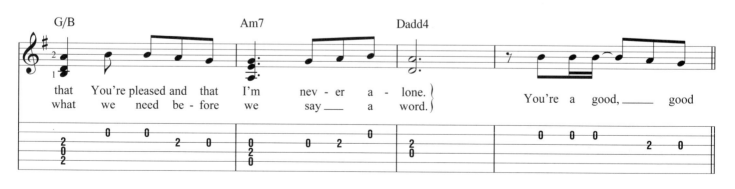

that You're pleased and that I'm nev-er a - lone.
what we need be - fore we say a word.
You're a good, good

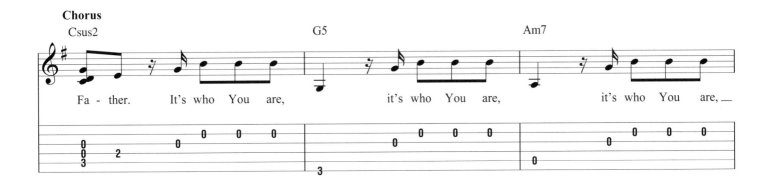

*2nd time, substitute G5

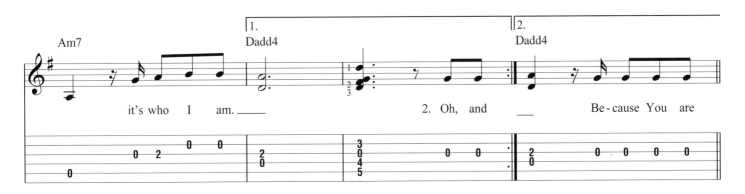

Bridge

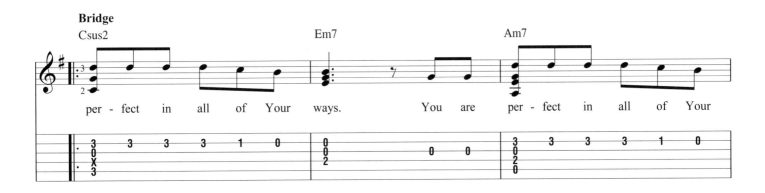

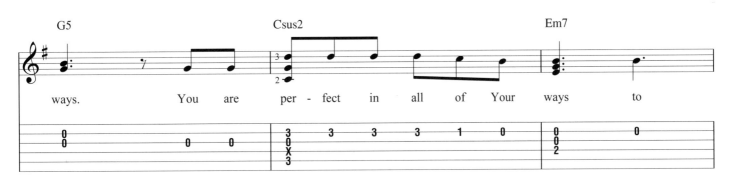

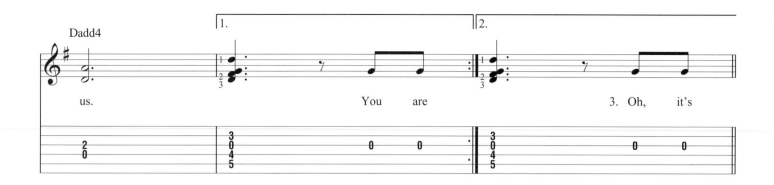

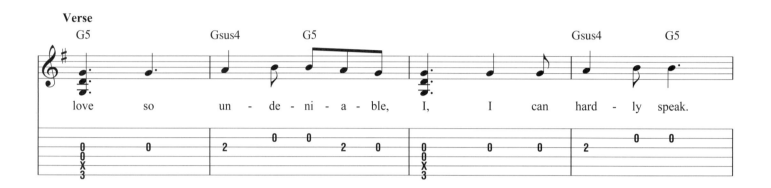

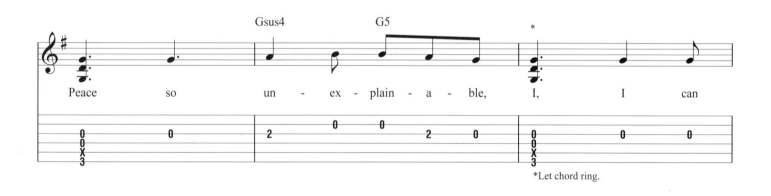

*Let chord ring.

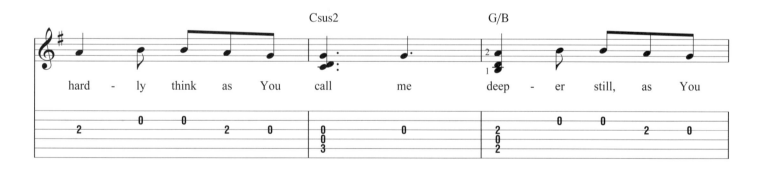

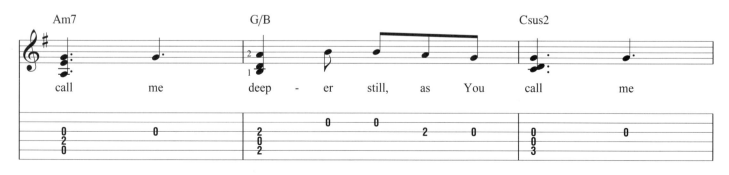

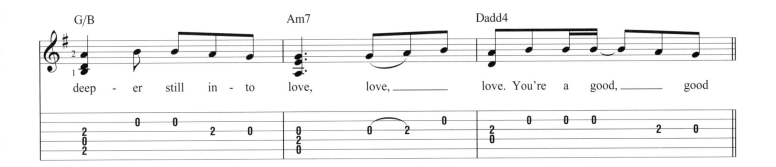

deep - er still in - to love, love, _____ love. You're a good, _____ good

Chorus

Fa - ther. It's who You are, it's who You are, it's who You are, __

__ and I'm loved __ by You. It's who I am, it's who I am,

it's who I am. __ You're a good, _____ good

Home

Words and Music by Chris Tomlin, Ed Cash and Scott Cash

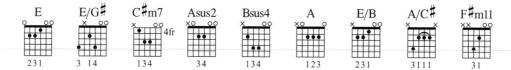

Strum Pattern: 5
Pick Pattern: 1

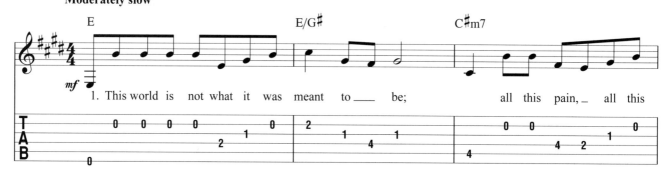

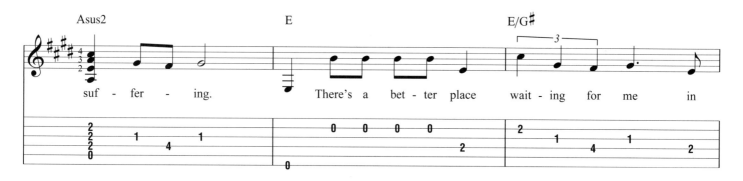

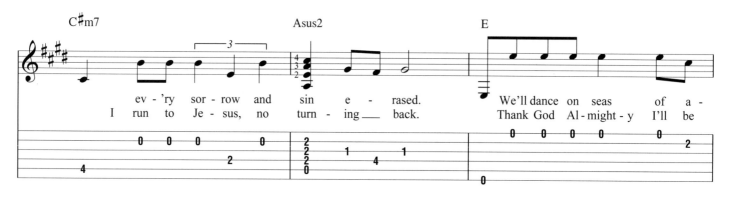

maz - ing   grace   in   heav - en, _____   in   heav - en. _____ I'm   go - ing
free   at   last   in   heav - en, _____   in   heav - en. _____

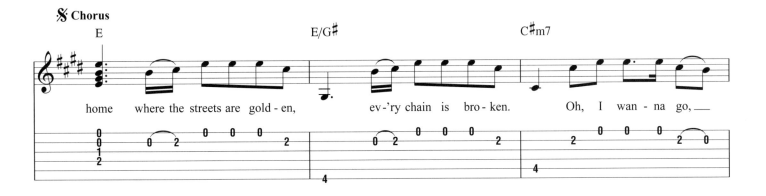

§ **Chorus**

home   where the streets are gold - en,   ev-'ry chain is bro - ken.   Oh,   I   wan - na go, ___

oh,   I   wan - na go ___ home,   where ev-'ry fear is gone,   I'm in Your o - pen arms

3rd time, To Coda ⊕ |1.

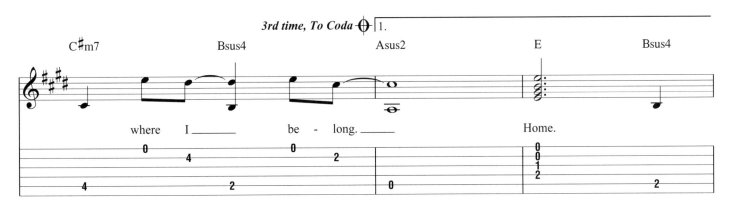

where   I _____   be - long. _____   Home.

|2.

Bridge

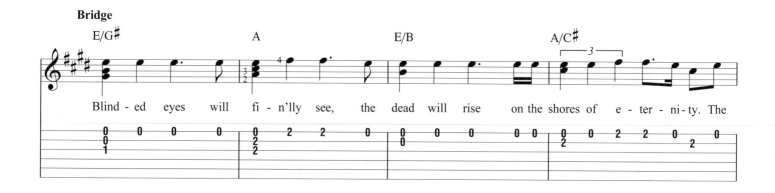

D.S. al Coda

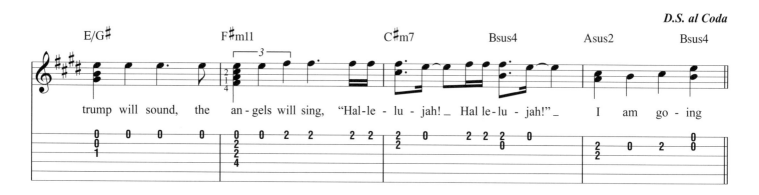

Coda

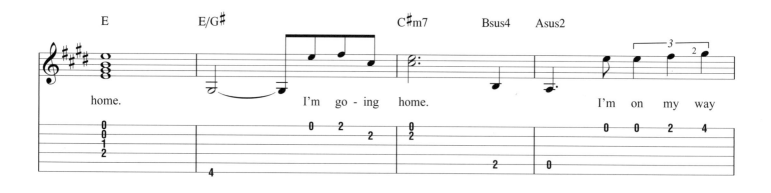

How Great Is Our God

Words and Music by Chris Tomlin, Jesse Reeves and Ed Cash

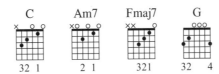

* Capo I

Strum Pattern: 4, 6
Pick Pattern: 4, 5

Intro
Moderately slow

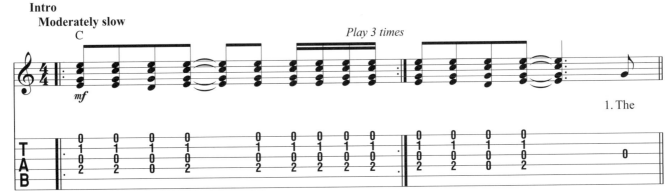

* Optional: To match recording, place capo at 1st fret.

Verse

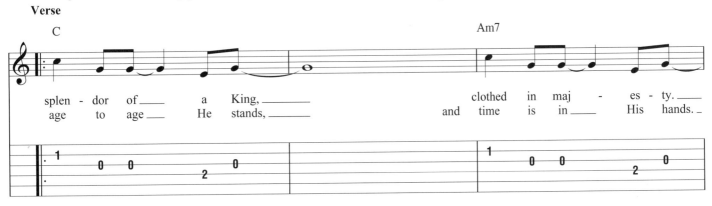

splen - dor of ___ a King, _____ clothed in maj - es - ty. ___
age to age ___ He stands, _____ and time is in ___ His hands. _

___ Let all the earth ___ re - joice, all the earth ___ re - joice. He wraps ___
Be - gin - ning and ___ the end, be - gin - ning and ___ the end. The God -

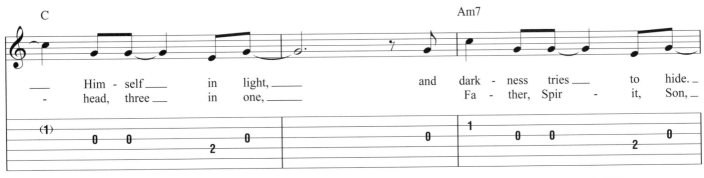

___ Him - self ___ in light, _____ and dark - ness tries ___ to hide. ___
- head, three ___ in one, _____ Fa - ther, Spir - it, Son, ___

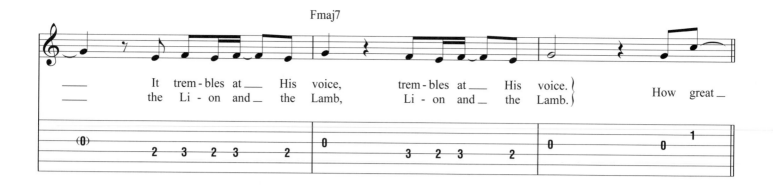

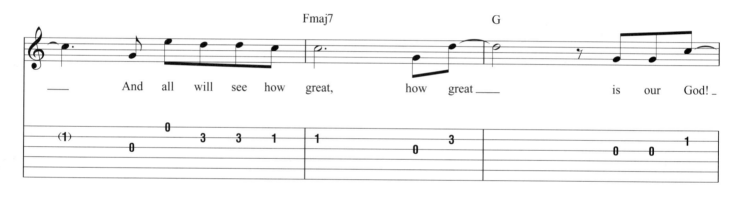

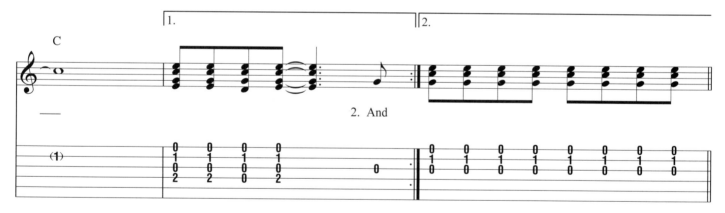

Bridge

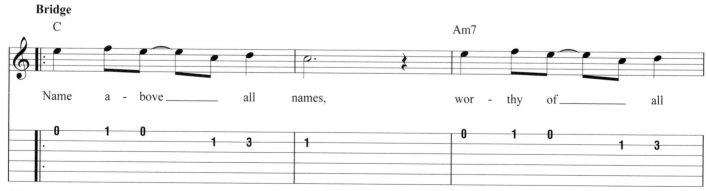

Outro-Chorus

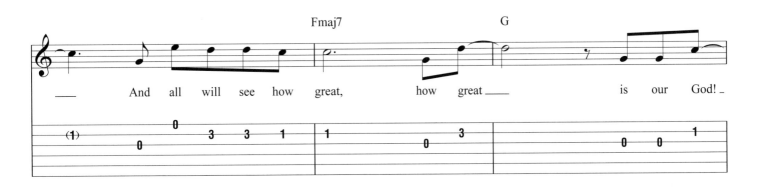

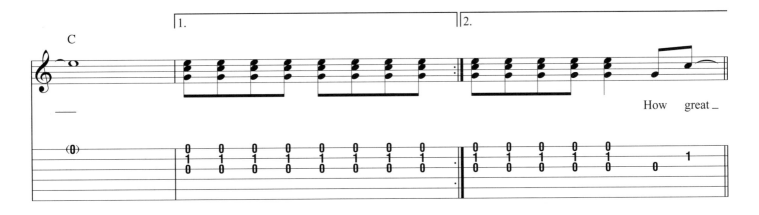

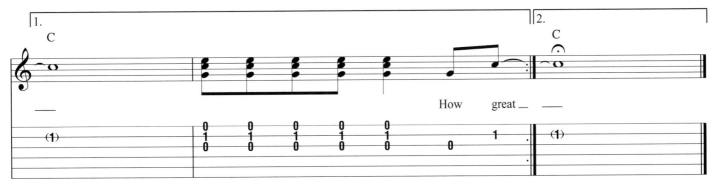

I Will Follow

Words and Music by Chris Tomlin, Reuben Morgan and Jason Ingram

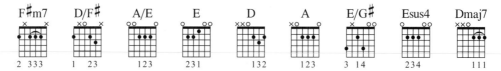

*Capo I

Strum Pattern: 3
Pick Pattern: 3

Intro-Chorus
Moderately slow

*Optional: To match recording, place capo at 1st fret.

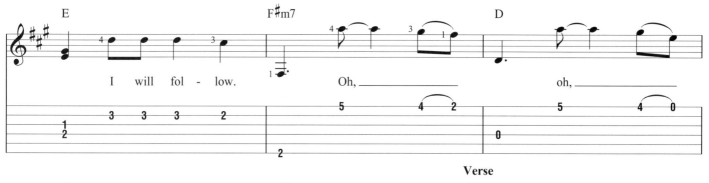

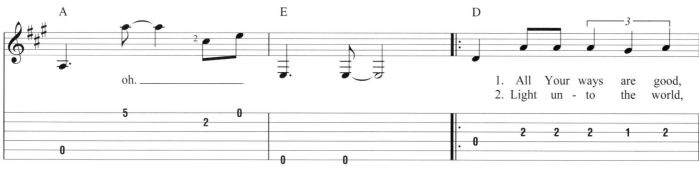

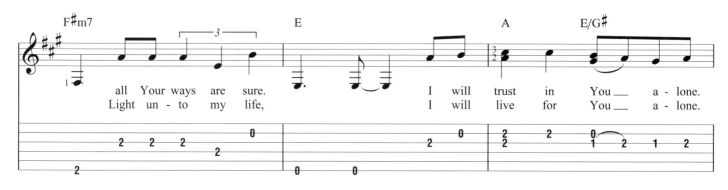

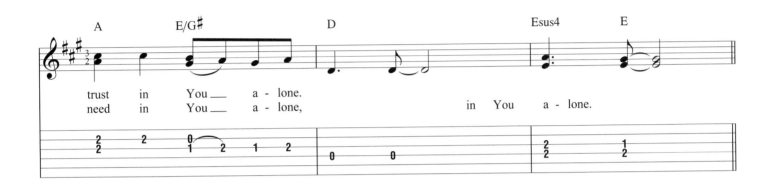

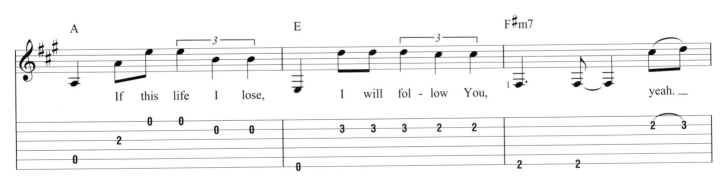

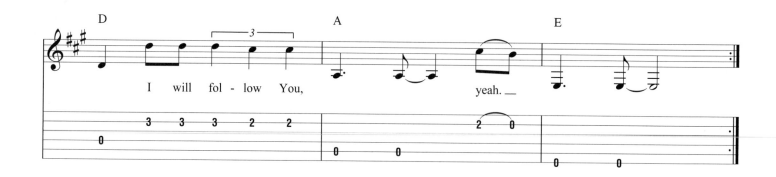

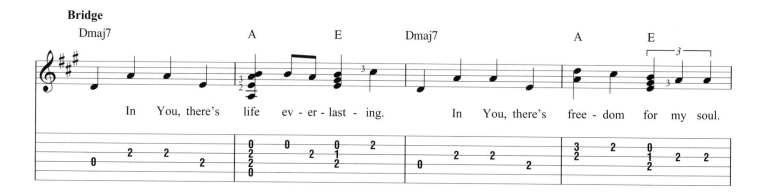

Bridge

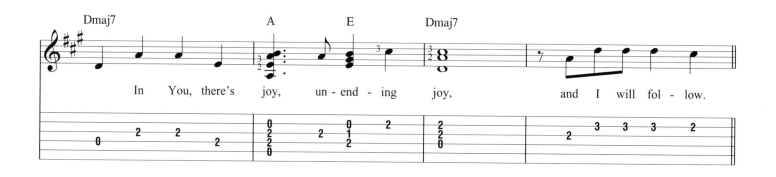

Chorus

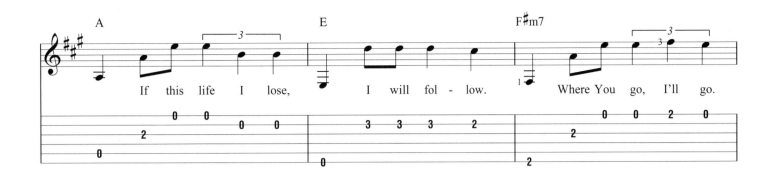

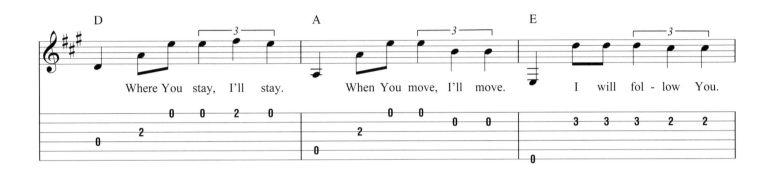

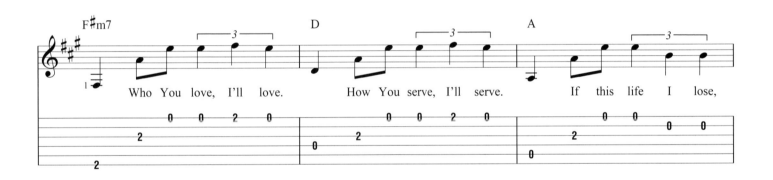

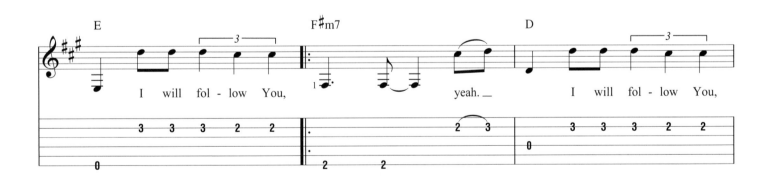

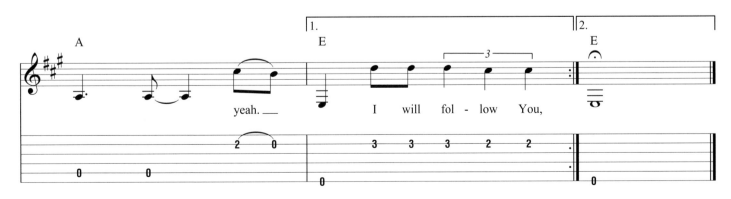

I Will Rise

Words and Music by Chris Tomlin, Jesse Reeves, Louie Giglio and Matt Maher

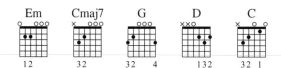

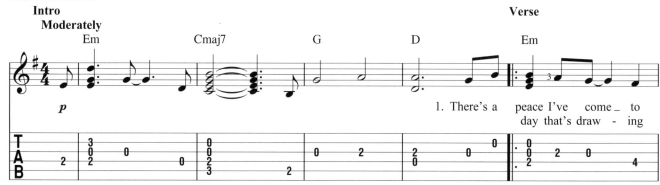

*Capo IV

Strum Pattern: 5
Pick Pattern: 4

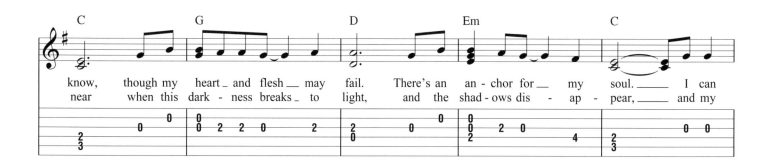

*Optional: To match recording, place capo at 4th fret.

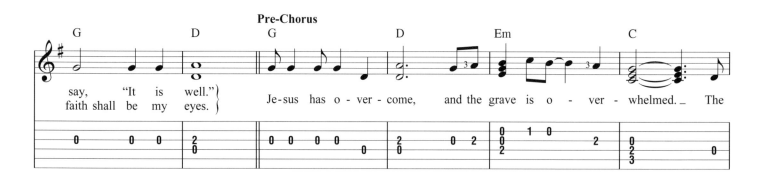

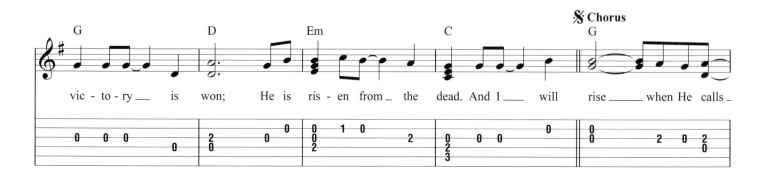

Jesus

Words and Music by Chris Tomlin and Ed Cash

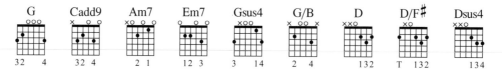

*Capo II

Strum Pattern: 5
Pick Pattern: 5

Verse
Moderately slow

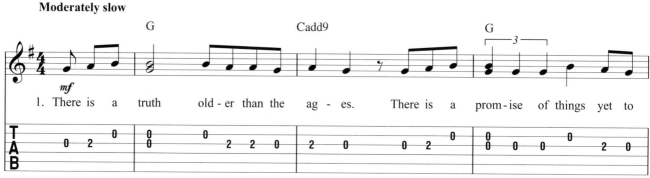

1. There is a truth old-er than the ag-es. There is a prom-ise of things yet to

*Optional: To match recording, place capo at 2nd fret.

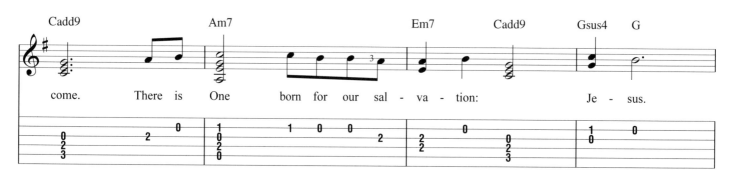

come. There is One born for our sal-va-tion: Je - sus.

Verse

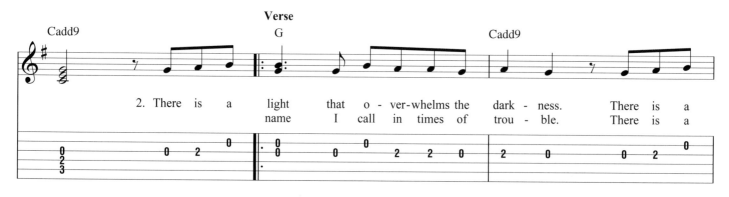

2. There is a light that o-ver-whelms the dark - ness. There is a
name I call in times of trou - ble. There is a

king - dom that for-ev-er reigns. There is free - dom from the chains that
song that com-forts in the night. There is a voice that calms the storm that

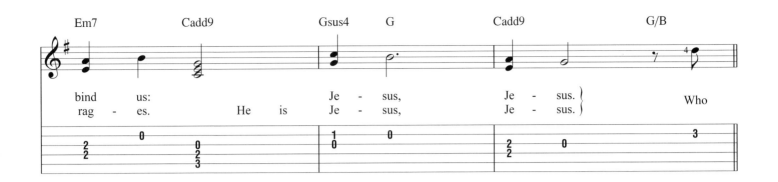

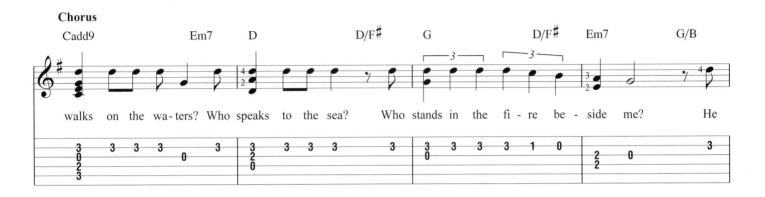

Chorus

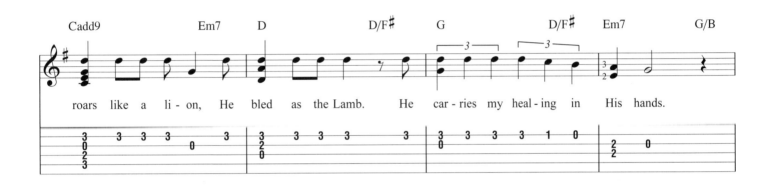

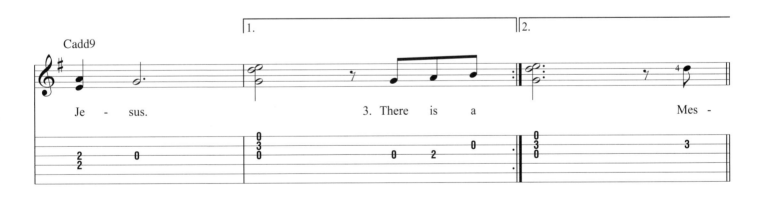

Bridge

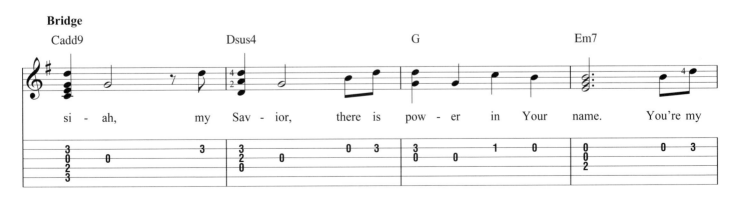

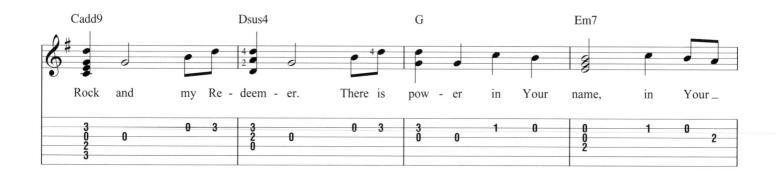

Rock and my Re - deem - er. There is pow - er in Your name, in Your _

Chorus

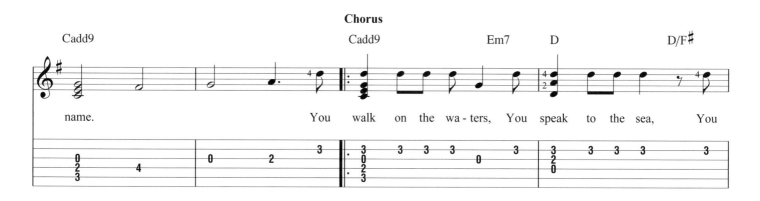

name. You walk on the wa - ters, You speak to the sea, You

stand in the fi - re be - side me. You roar like a li - on, You bled as the Lamb. You

car - ried my heal - ing in Your hands. God, You Your hands. Je - sus.

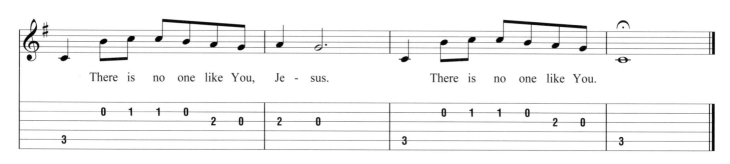

There is no one like You, Je - sus. There is no one like You.

Our God

Words and Music by Jonas Myrin, Chris Tomlin, Matt Redman and Jesse Reeves

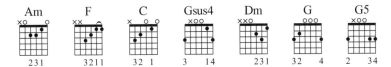

*Tune down 1/2 step:
(low to high) Eb-Ab-Db-Gb-Bb-Eb

Strum Pattern: 1
Pick Pattern: 5

Intro
Moderately

*Optional: To match recording, tune down 1/2 step.

Verse

1. Wa - ter You turned ___ in - to wine, ___

o - pened the eyes ___ of the blind. ___ There's no one like You,

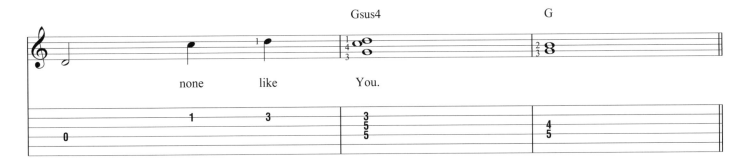

none like You.

Verse

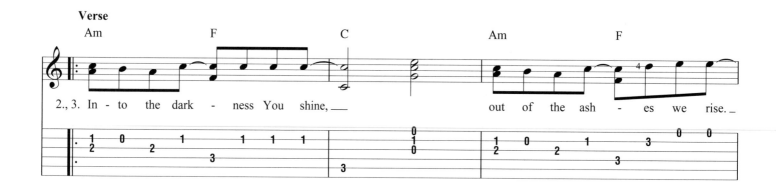

2., 3. In - to the dark - ness You shine, ___ out of the ash - es we rise. ___

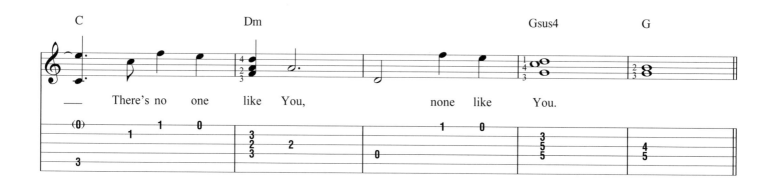

___ There's no one like You, none like You.

Chorus

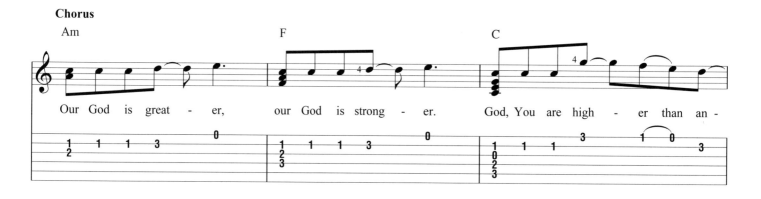

Our God is great - er, our God is strong - er. God, You are high - er than an -

- y oth - er. Our God is Heal - er, awe - some in pow - er, our ___

1.

Interlude

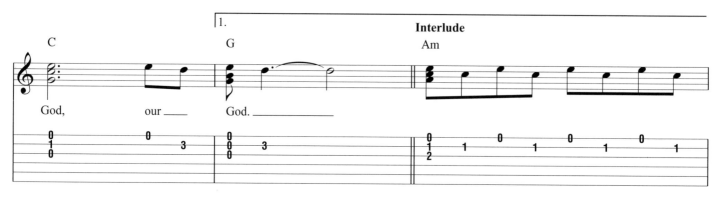

God, our ___ God. _____

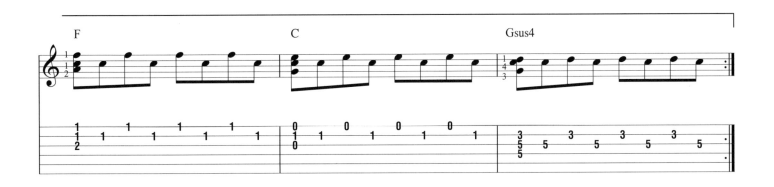

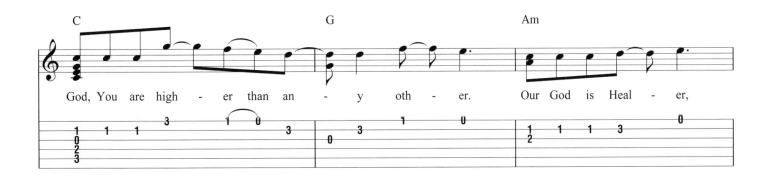

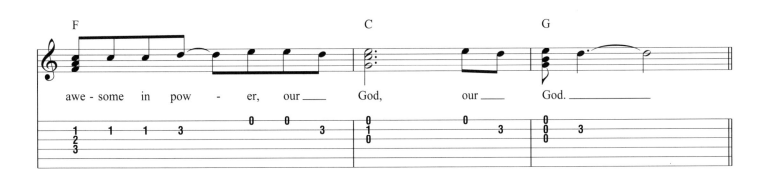

Interlude

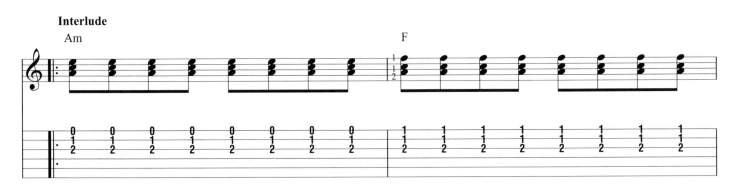

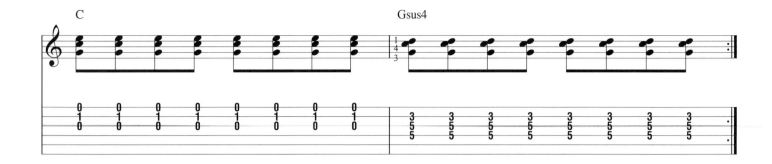

%. Bridge

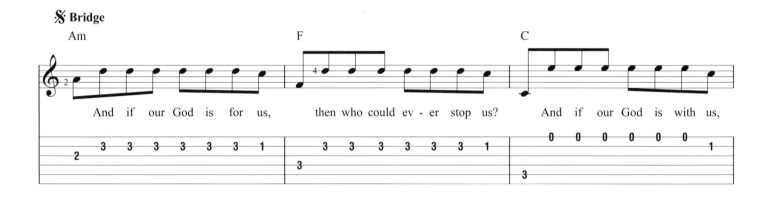

And if our God is for us, then who could ev - er stop us? And if our God is with us,

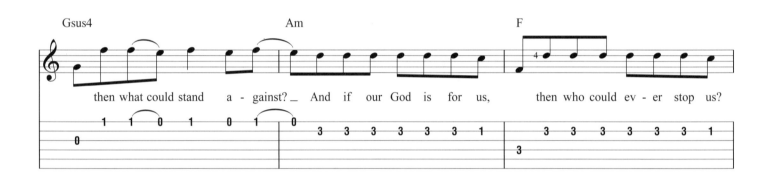

then what could stand a - gainst? _ And if our God is for us, then who could ev - er stop us?

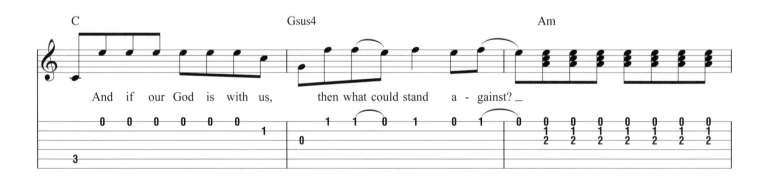

And if our God is with us, then what could stand a - gainst? _

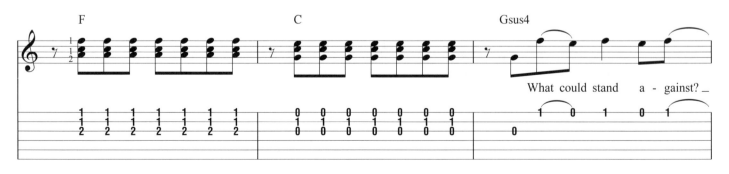

What could stand a - gainst? _

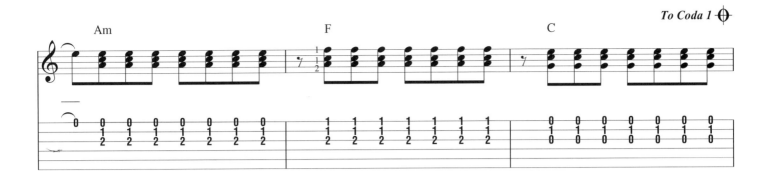

%% **Chorus**

*3rd & 4th times, **Slower***

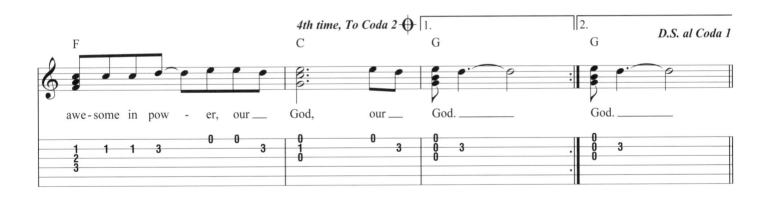

4th time, To Coda 2 ⊕ |1. ||2.   *D.S. al Coda 1*

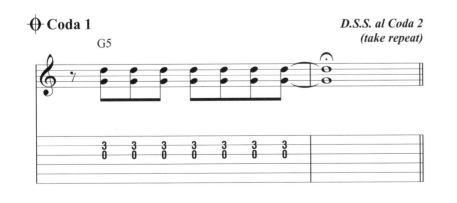

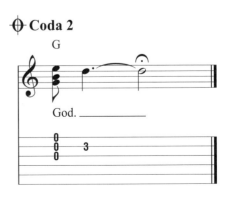

Jesus Messiah

Words and Music by Chris Tomlin, Jesse Reeves, Daniel Carson and Ed Cash

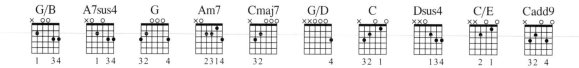

*Capo IV

Strum Pattern: 5
Pick Pattern: 5

Intro
Moderately slow

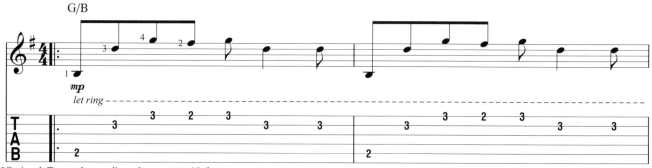

*Optional: To match recording, place capo at 4th fret.

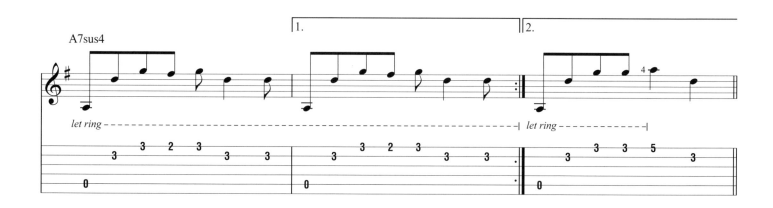

Verse

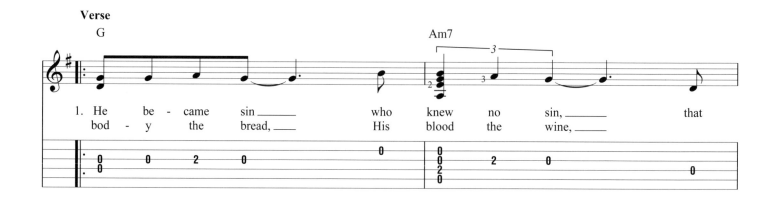

1. He be-came sin _____ who knew no sin, _____ that
bod-y the bread, _____ His blood the wine, _____

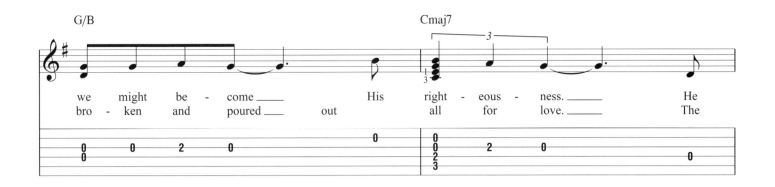

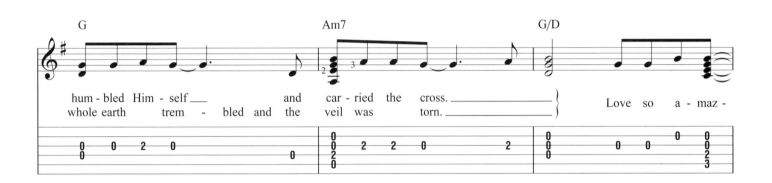

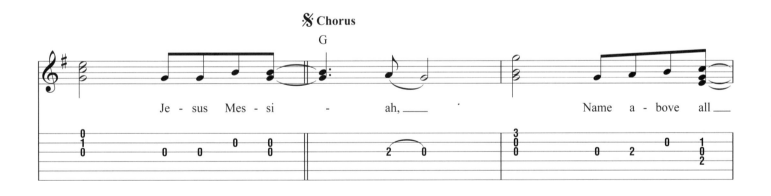

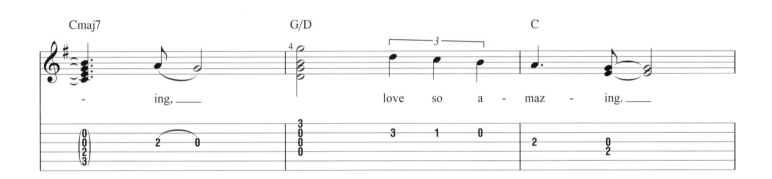

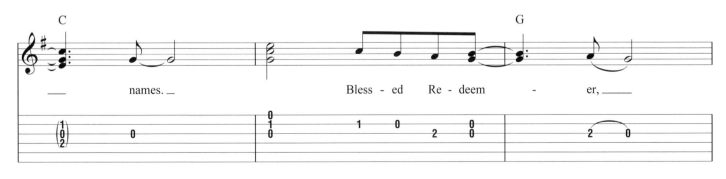

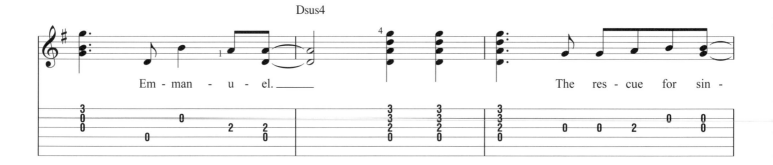

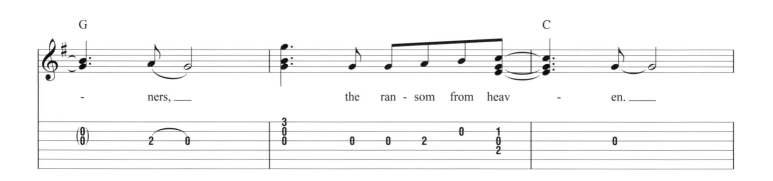

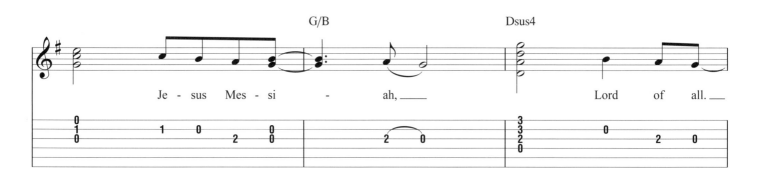

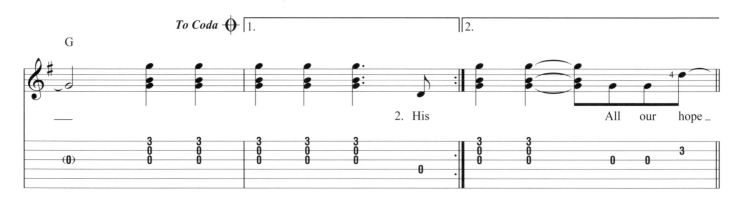

Bridge

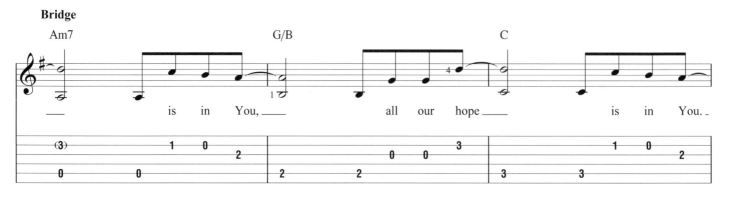

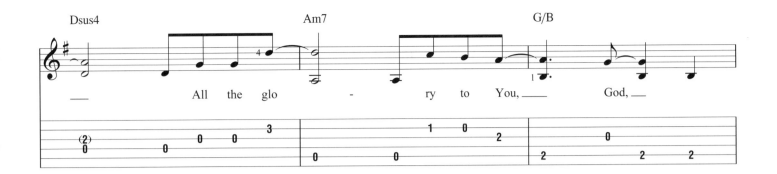

D.S. al Coda

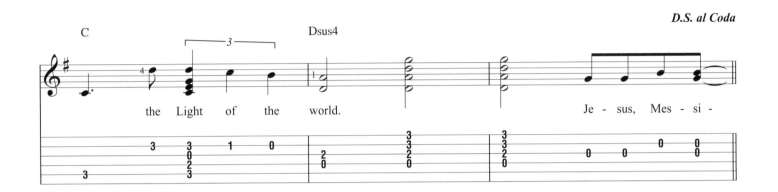

Coda

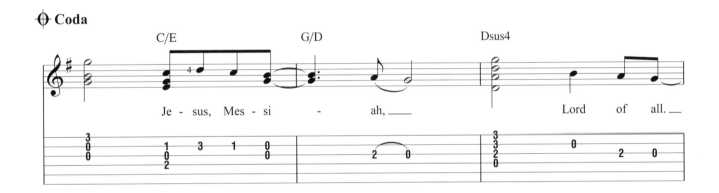

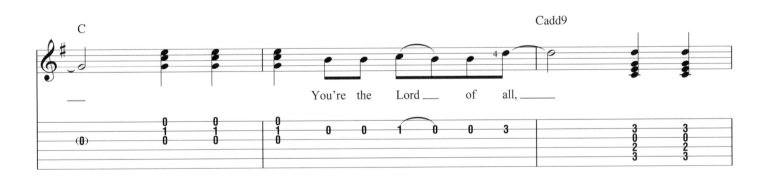

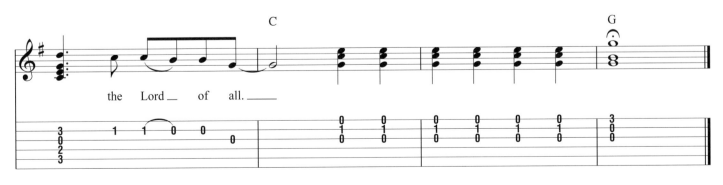

We Fall Down

Words and Music by Chris Tomlin

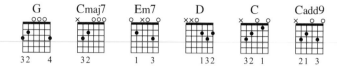

*Tune down 1/2 step:
(low to high) E♭-A♭-D♭-G♭-B♭-E♭

Strum Pattern: 1
Pick Pattern: 5

Intro
Moderately slow

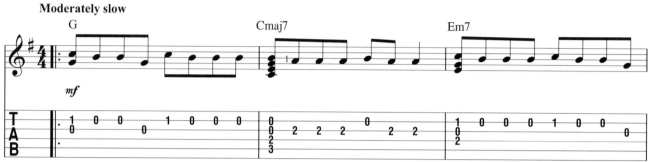

*Optional: To match recording, tune down 1/2 step.

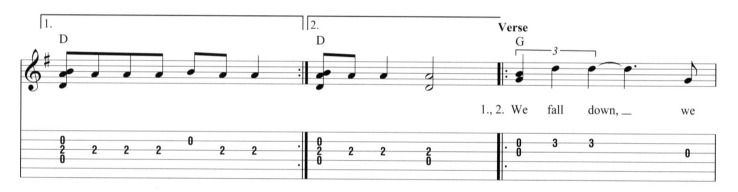

1., 2. We fall down, __ we

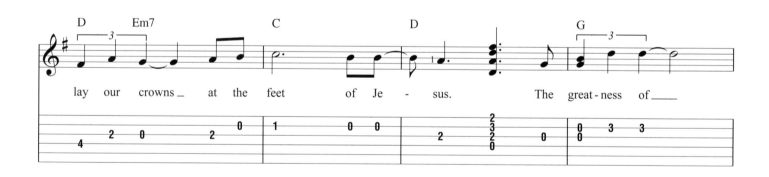

lay our crowns __ at the feet of Je - sus. The great-ness of __

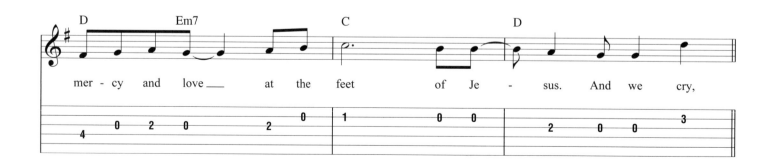

mer - cy and love __ at the feet of Je - sus. And we cry,

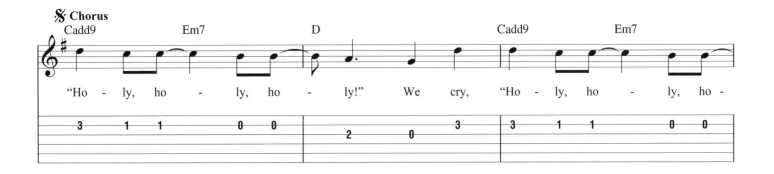

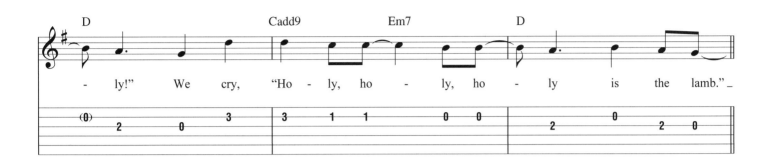

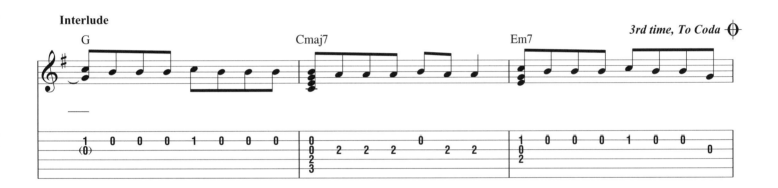

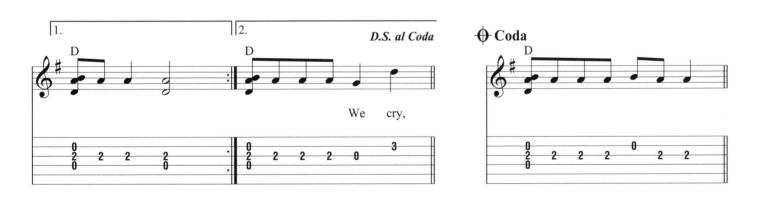

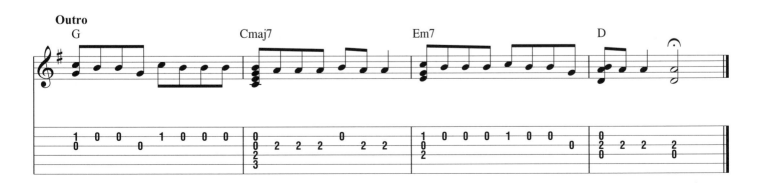

Whom Shall I Fear
(God of Angel Armies)

Words and Music by Chris Tomlin, Ed Cash and Scott Cash

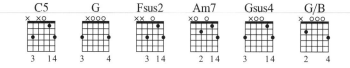

Strum Pattern: 1
Pick Pattern: 5

Intro
Slow

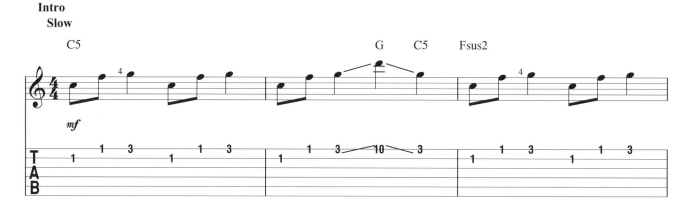

Verse

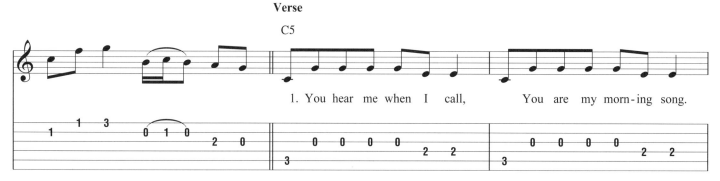

1. You hear me when I call, You are my morn-ing song.

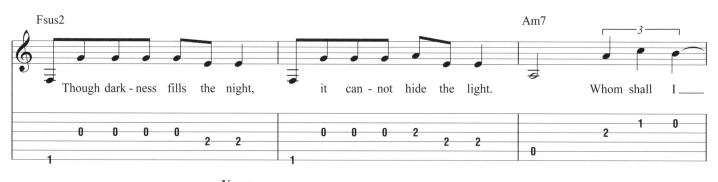

Though dark-ness fills the night, it can-not hide the light. Whom shall I ___

Verse

___ fear? ___ 2. You crush the en-e-my un-der-neath my feet.

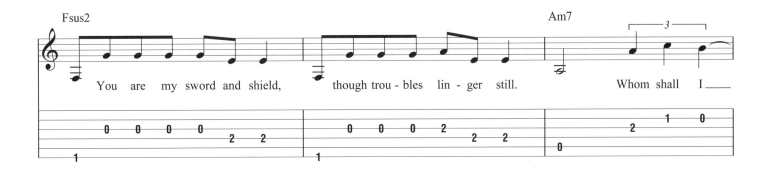

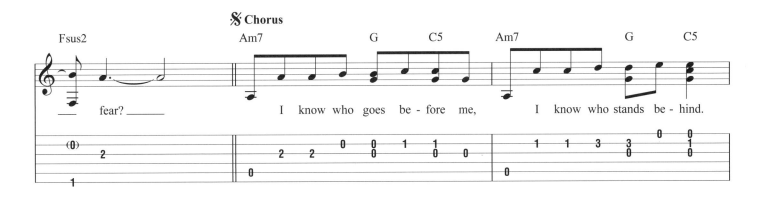

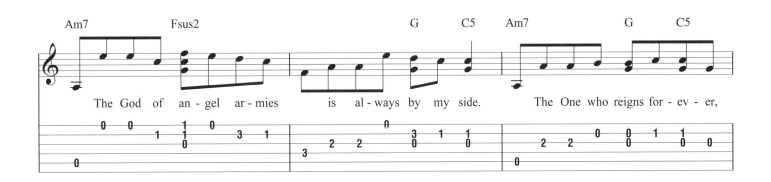

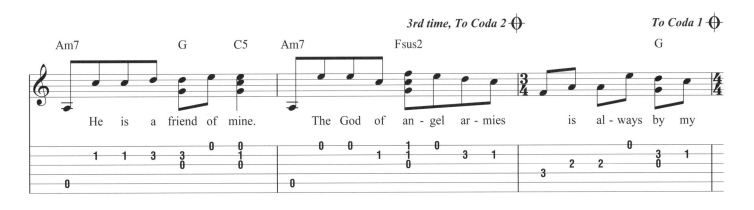

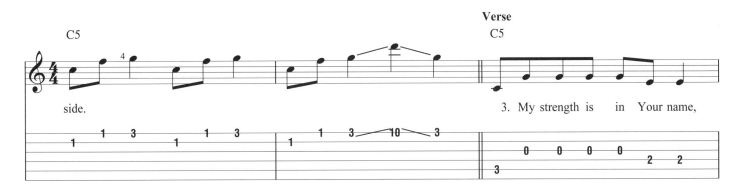

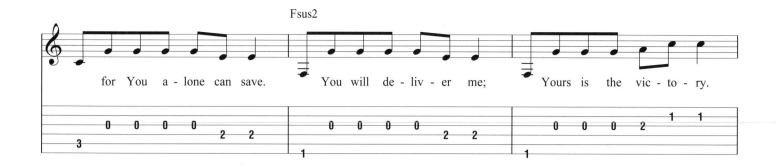

Fsus2

for You a - lone can save. You will de - liv - er me; Yours is the vic - to - ry.

D.S. al Coda 1

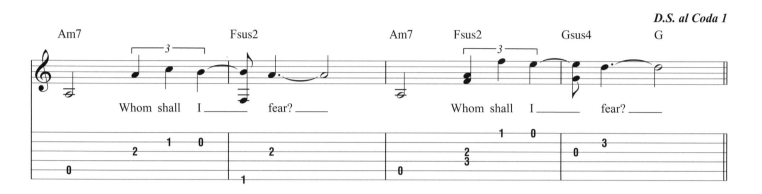

Am7   Fsus2   Am7   Fsus2   Gsus4   G

Whom shall I _____ fear? _____   Whom shall I _____ fear? _____

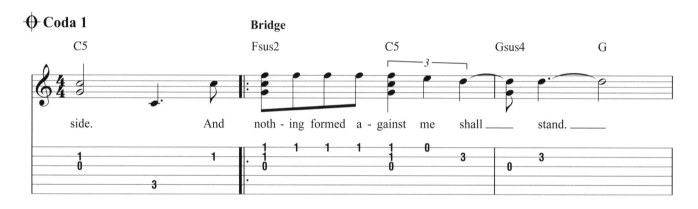

⊕ **Coda 1**   **Bridge**

C5   Fsus2   C5   Gsus4   G

side.   And noth - ing formed a - gainst me shall ____ stand. _____

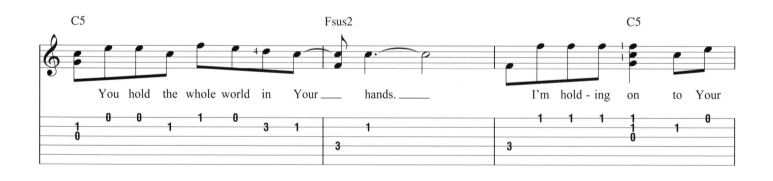

C5   Fsus2   C5

You hold the whole world in Your ___ hands. _____   I'm hold - ing on to Your

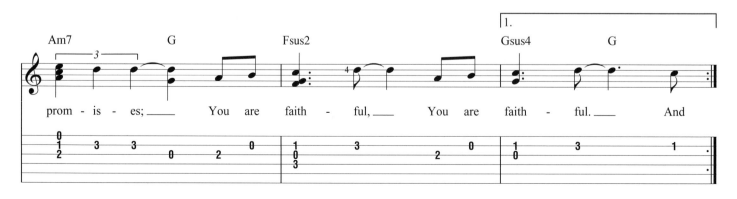

Am7   G   Fsus2   Gsus4   G   1.

prom - is - es; _____ You are faith - ful, _____ You are faith - ful. ____ And

faith - ful, _____ You are faith - ful. _____

Coda 2

Outro-Chorus

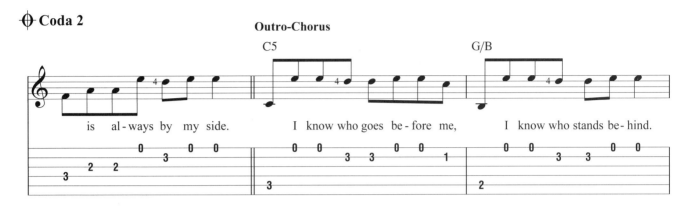

is al-ways by my side. I know who goes be-fore me, I know who stands be-hind.

The God of an-gel ar-mies is al-ways by my side. The One who reigns for-ev-er,

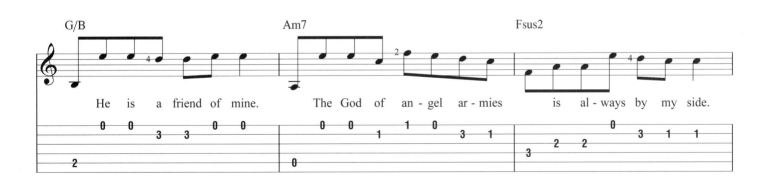

He is a friend of mine. The God of an-gel ar-mies is al-ways by my side.

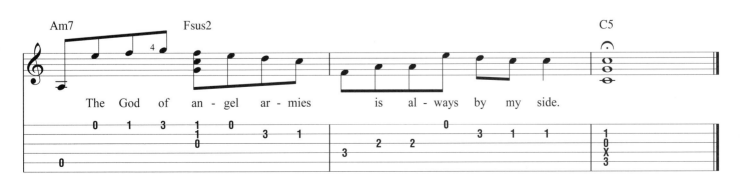

The God of an-gel ar-mies is al-ways by my side.

The Wonderful Cross

Words and Music by Jesse Reeves, Chris Tomlin and J.D. Walt

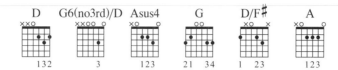

Strum Pattern: 3, 4
Pick Pattern: 2, 5

Verse

Moderately slow

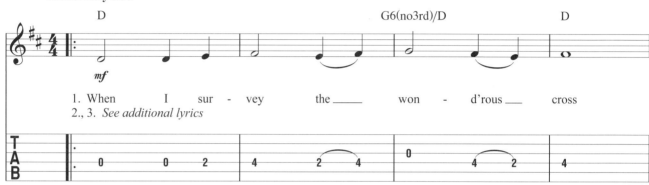

1. When I sur-vey the ____ won - d'rous ____ cross
2., 3. *See additional lyrics*

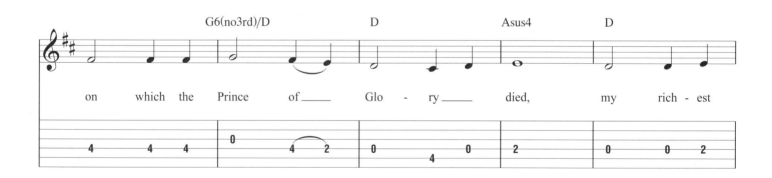

on which the Prince of ____ Glo - ry ____ died, my rich - est

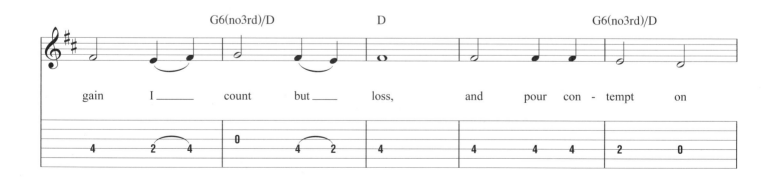

gain I ____ count but ____ loss, and pour con - tempt on

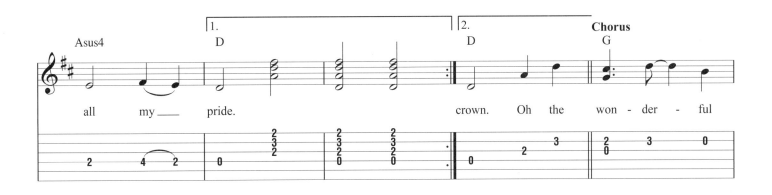

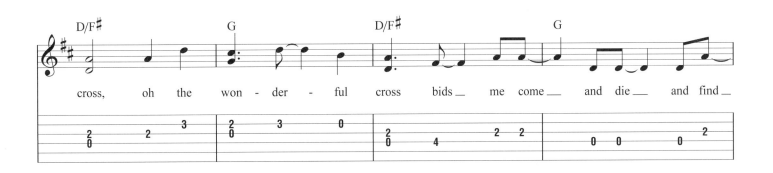

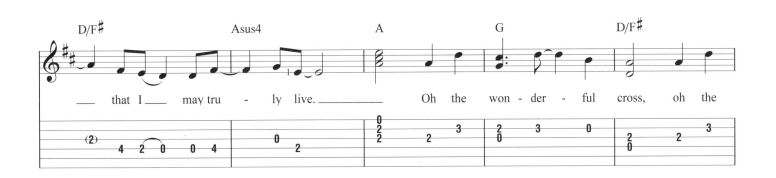

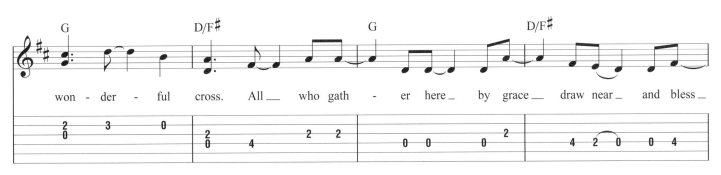

To Coda ⊕

D.C. al Coda
(take 2nd ending)

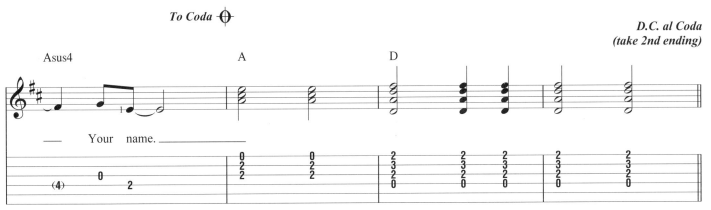

⊕ **Coda**

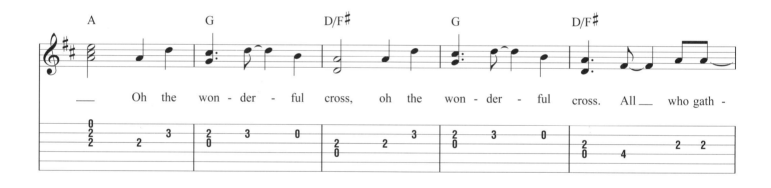

Additional Lyrics

2. See from His head, His hands, His feet,
   Sorrow and love flow mingled down.
   Did e'er such love and sorrow meet,
   Or thorns compose so rich a crown?

3. Were the whole realm of nature mine,
   That were an offering far too small.
   Love so amazing, so divine,
   Demands my soul, my life, my all.

CHRISTIAN SONGBOOKS
FOR EASY GUITAR

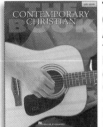

THE CONTEMPORARY CHRISTIAN BOOK
A huge collection of 85 CCM favorites arranged for beginning-level guitarists. Includes: Abba (Father) • Above All • Awesome God • Beautiful • Dive • Friends • His Eyes • How Great Is Our God • Jesus Freak • Lifesong • Mountain of God • This Is Your Time • Wholly Yours • Word of God Speak • and more.
00702195 Easy Guitar (No Tab)........................$17.99

THE CONTEMPORARY CHRISTIAN COLLECTION
INCLUDES TAB Easy arrangements of 50 Christian hits, complete with tab! Includes: Alive Again • All Because of Jesus • Beautiful • Big House • By Your Side • Dive • Enough • Give Me Your Eyes • Hold My Heart • Joy • Live Out Loud • More • Song of Hope • Undo • Wholly Yours • The Word Is Alive • and dozens more!
00702283 Easy Guitar with Notes & Tab.........$16.99

4-CHORD WORSHIP SONGS FOR GUITAR
PLAY 25 WORSHIP SONGS WITH FOUR CHORDS: G-C-D-Em More than two dozen Christian hits that guitarists can play using just four chords! Includes: All We Need • Ancient Words • Awesome God • Breathe • Everyday • Forever • I Will Rise • Love the Lord • No One like You • Unchanging • more!
00701727 Guitar Chords...................................$10.99

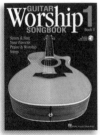

GUITAR WORSHIP METHOD SONGBOOK BOOK 1
Book/CD Pack This book can be used on its own, as a supplement to *Guitar Worship Method Book 1* (00695681) or with any other guitar method. You get lyrics, chord frames, strumming patterns, and a full-band CD, so you can hear how each song sounds and then play along when you're ready. Songs include: Better Is One Day • Blessed Be Your Name • Breathe • Forever • Here I Am to Worship • I Could Sing of Your Love Forever • Lord, Reign in Me • You Are My King (Amazing Love).
00699641 Lyrics/Chord Frames $14.99

GUITAR WORSHIP METHOD SONGBOOK 2
INCLUDES TAB *Book/CD Pack* 12 more songs with lyrics, chord frames, strumming patterns and a full-band CD that you can use for your worship-playing needs. Songs include: Awesome God • Enough • Give Us Clean Hands • God of Wonders • The Heart of Worship • How Great Is Our God • In Christ Alone • Mighty to Save • Shout to the Lord • Sing to the King • Step by Step • We Fall Down.
00701082 Guitar Arrangements $14.99

PRAISE AND WORSHIP FOR GUITAR
INCLUDES TAB Easy arrangements of 45 beautiful Praise and Worship songs, including: As the Deer • Be Not Afraid • Emmanuel • Glorify Thy Name • Great Is the Lord • He Is Exalted • Holy Ground • Lamb of God • Majesty • Thou Art Worthy • We Bow Down • You Are My Hiding Place • and more.
00702125 Easy Guitar with Notes & Tab.........$10.99

3-CHORD WORSHIP SONGS FOR GUITAR
PLAY 24 WORSHIP SONGS WITH THREE CHORDS: G-C-D Two dozen tunes playable on guitar using only G, C and D chords. Includes: Agnus Dei • Because We Believe • Enough • Father I Adore You • Here I Am to Worship • Step by Step • There Is a Redeemer • We Fall Down • Worthy, You Are Worthy • and more. No tab.
00701131 Guitar Chords................................$10.99

TOP WORSHIP HITS
INCLUDES TAB Easier arrangements perfect for guitarists who want to join in the worship service. Includes 30 songs: Beautiful One • Blessed Be Your Name • God of Wonders • Hosanna (Praise Is Rising) • I Give You My Heart • Mighty to Save • Revelation Song • Sing to the King • Your Grace Is Enough • and more.
00702294 Easy Guitar with Notes & Tab.........$15.99

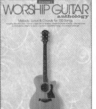

THE WORSHIP BOOK
Easy arrangements (no tab) of 80 great worship tunes, including: Above All • Days of Elijah • Forever • Here I Am to Worship • Mighty to Save • Open the Eyes of My Heart • Shout to the Lord • Sing to the King • We Fall Down • and more.
00702247 Easy Guitar (No Tab)......................$15.99

THE WORSHIP GUITAR ANTHOLOGY – VOLUME 1
This collection contains melody, lyrics & chords for 100 contemporary favorites, such as: Beautiful One • Forever • Here I Am to Worship • Hosanna (Praise Is Rising) • How He Loves • In Christ Alone • Mighty to Save • Our God • Revelation Song • Your Grace Is Enough • and dozens more.
00101864 Melody/Lyrics/Chords....................$16.99

CHORDBUDDY GUITAR LEARNING SYSTEM – WORSHIP EDITION
ChordBuddy Media As soon as the ChordBuddy is properly attached to your acoustic or electric guitar, you will be able to make music instantly. Within a few weeks, you'll begin removing some of the tabs and making the chords on your own. In two months, you'll be able to play the guitar with no ChordBuddy at all! Package Includes: ChordBuddy • instruction book • companion DVD with a 2-month lesson plan • and ChordBuddy songbook with 60 songs. This Worship Edition uses songs in both the songbook and instructional book that are geared for Sunday school, praise and worship bands, and more.
00124638 Songbook with ChordBuddy Device & DVD...........................$49.95

CHORDBUDDY WORSHIP SONGBOOK
ChordBuddy Media This songbook includes 60 timeless Christian tunes in color-coded arrangements that correspond to the device colors: Awesome God • Because of Your Love • Create in Me a Clean Heart • I Could Sing of Your Love Forever • Jesus Loves Me • Kum Ba Yah • More Precious Than Silver • Rock of Ages • Shout to the North • This Little Light of Mine • and more. ChordBuddy device is sold separately.
00127895 Book Only $14.99

HAL•LEONARD®
www.halleonard.com

Prices, contents and availability subject to change without notice.

0917

EASY GUITAR
WITH NOTES & TAB

This series features simplified arrangements with notes, tab, chord charts, and strum and pick patterns.

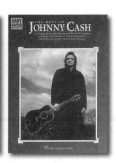

MIXED FOLIOS

00702287	Acoustic	$14.99
00702002	Acoustic Rock Hits for Easy Guitar	$14.99
00702166	All-Time Best Guitar Collection	$19.99
00699665	Beatles Best	$14.99
00702232	Best Acoustic Songs for Easy Guitar	$14.99
00119835	Best Children's Songs	$16.99
00702233	Best Hard Rock Songs	$14.99
00703055	The Big Book of Nursery Rhymes & Children's Songs	$14.99
00322179	The Big Easy Book of Classic Rock Guitar	$24.95
00698978	Big Christmas Collection	$16.95
00702394	Bluegrass Songs for Easy Guitar	$12.99
00703387	Celtic Classics	$14.99
00224808	Chart Hits of 2016-2017	$14.99
00156245	Chart Hits of 2015-2016	$14.99
00702149	Children's Christian Songbook	$9.99
00702237	Christian Acoustic Favorites	$12.95
00702028	Christmas Classics	$8.99
00101779	Christmas Guitar	$14.99
00702185	Christmas Hits	$9.95
00702141	Classic Rock	$8.95
00702203	CMT's 100 Greatest Country Songs	$27.95
00702283	The Contemporary Christian Collection	$16.99
00702239	Country Classics for Easy Guitar	$19.99
00702282	Country Hits of 2009–2010	$14.99
00702257	Easy Acoustic Guitar Songs	$14.99
00702280	Easy Guitar Tab White Pages	$29.99
00702041	Favorite Hymns for Easy Guitar	$10.99
00140841	4-Chord Hymns for Guitar	$7.99
00702281	4 Chord Rock	$10.99
00126894	Frozen	$14.99
00702286	Glee	$16.99
00699374	Gospel Favorites	$14.95
00122138	The Grammy Awards® Record of the Year 1958-2011	$19.99
00702160	The Great American Country Songbook	$16.99
00702050	Great Classical Themes for Easy Guitar	$8.99
00702116	Greatest Hymns for Guitar	$10.99
00702130	The Groovy Years	$9.95
00702184	Guitar Instrumentals	$9.95
00148030	Halloween Guitar Songs	$14.99
00702273	Irish Songs	$12.99
00702275	Jazz Favorites for Easy Guitar	$15.99
00702274	Jazz Standards for Easy Guitar	$15.99
00702162	Jumbo Easy Guitar Songbook	$19.99
00702258	Legends of Rock	$14.99
00702261	Modern Worship Hits	$14.99
00702189	MTV's 100 Greatest Pop Songs	$24.95
00702272	1950s Rock	$15.99
00702271	1960s Rock	$15.99
00702270	1970s Rock	$15.99
00702269	1980s Rock	$14.99
00702268	1990s Rock	$14.99
00109725	Once	$14.99
00702187	Selections from O Brother Where Art Thou?	$14.99
00702178	100 Songs for Kids	$14.99
00702515	Pirates of the Caribbean	$12.99
00702125	Praise and Worship for Guitar	$10.99
00702285	Southern Rock Hits	$12.99
00121535	30 Easy Celtic Guitar Solos	$14.99
00702220	Today's Country Hits	$9.95
00121900	Today's Women of Pop & Rock	$14.99
00702294	Top Worship Hits	$15.99
00702255	VH1's 100 Greatest Hard Rock Songs	$27.95
00702175	VH1's 100 Greatest Songs of Rock and Roll	$24.95
00702253	Wicked	$12.99

ARTIST COLLECTIONS

00702267	AC/DC for Easy Guitar	$15.99
00702598	Adele for Easy Guitar	$15.99
00702040	Best of the Allman Brothers	$14.99
00702865	J.S. Bach for Easy Guitar	$14.99
00702169	Best of The Beach Boys	$12.99
00702292	The Beatles — 1	$19.99
00125796	Best of Chuck Berry	$14.99
00702201	The Essential Black Sabbath	$12.95
02501615	Zac Brown Band — The Foundation	$16.99
02501621	Zac Brown Band — You Get What You Give	$16.99
00702043	Best of Johnny Cash	$16.99
00702263	Best of Casting Crowns	$14.99
00702090	Eric Clapton's Best	$10.95
00702086	Eric Clapton — from the Album Unplugged	$10.95
00702202	The Essential Eric Clapton	$14.99
00702250	blink-182 — Greatest Hits	$15.99
00702053	Best of Patsy Cline	$12.99
00702229	The Very Best of Creedence Clearwater Revival	$15.99
00702145	Best of Jim Croce	$15.99
00702278	Crosby, Stills & Nash	$12.99
00702219	David Crowder*Band Collection	$12.95
14042809	Bob Dylan	$14.99
00702276	Fleetwood Mac — Easy Guitar Collection	$14.99
00130952	Foo Fighters	$14.99
00139462	The Very Best of Grateful Dead	$14.99
00702136	Best of Merle Haggard	$12.99
00702227	Jimi Hendrix — Smash Hits	$14.99
00702288	Best of Hillsong United	$12.99
00702236	Best of Antonio Carlos Jobim	$12.95
00702245	Elton John — Greatest Hits 1970–2002	$14.99
00129855	Jack Johnson	$14.99
00702204	Robert Johnson	$10.99
00702234	Selections from Toby Keith — 35 Biggest Hits	$12.95
00702003	Kiss	$10.99
00110578	Best of Kutless	$12.99
00702216	Lynyrd Skynyrd	$15.99
00702182	The Essential Bob Marley	$12.95
00146081	Maroon 5	$14.99
00121925	Bruno Mars – Unorthodox Jukebox	$12.99
00702248	Paul McCartney — All the Best	$14.99
00702129	Songs of Sarah McLachlan	$12.95
00125484	The Best of MercyMe	$12.99
02501316	Metallica — Death Magnetic	$17.99
00702209	Steve Miller Band — Young Hearts (Greatest Hits)	$12.95
00124167	Jason Mraz	$14.99
00702096	Best of Nirvana	$15.99
00702211	The Offspring — Greatest Hits	$12.95
00138026	One Direction	$14.99
00702030	Best of Roy Orbison	$12.95
00702144	Best of Ozzy Osbourne	$14.99
00702279	Tom Petty	$12.99
00102911	Pink Floyd	$16.99
00702139	Elvis Country Favorites	$12.99
00702293	The Very Best of Prince	$14.99
00699415	Best of Queen for Guitar	$14.99
00109279	Best of R.E.M.	$14.99
00702208	Red Hot Chili Peppers — Greatest Hits	$12.95
00174793	The Very Best of Santana	$14.99
00702196	Best of Bob Seger	$12.95
00146046	Ed Sheeran	$14.99
00702252	Frank Sinatra — Nothing But the Best	$12.99
00702010	Best of Rod Stewart	$16.99
00702049	Best of George Strait	$14.99
00702259	Taylor Swift for Easy Guitar	$15.99
00702260	Taylor Swift — Fearless	$14.99
00139727	Taylor Swift — 1989	$17.99
00115960	Taylor Swift — Red	$16.99
00702290	Taylor Swift — Speak Now	$15.99
00702226	Chris Tomlin — See the Morning	$12.95
00148643	Train	$14.99
00702427	U2 — 18 Singles	$14.99
00102711	Van Halen	$16.99
00702108	Best of Stevie Ray Vaughan	$14.99
00702123	Best of Hank Williams	$14.99
00702111	Stevie Wonder — Guitar Collection	$9.95
00702228	Neil Young — Greatest Hits	$15.99
00119133	Neil Young — Harvest	$14.99
00702188	Essential ZZ Top	$10.95

Prices, contents and availability subject to change without notice.

HAL•LEONARD®

Visit Hal Leonard online at
www.halleonard.com

0917

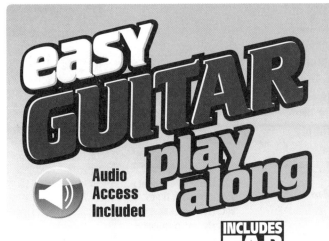

easy GUITAR play along

Audio Access Included

INCLUDES TAB

The ***Easy Guitar Play Along***® series features streamlined transcriptions of your favorite songs. Just follow the tab, listen to the audio to hear how the guitar should sound, and then play along using the backing tracks. Playback tools are provided for slowing down the tempo without changing pitch and looping challenging parts. The melody and lyrics are included in the book so that you can sing or simply follow along.

1. ROCK CLASSICS

Jailbreak • Living After Midnight • Mississippi Queen • Rocks Off • Runnin' Down a Dream • Smoke on the Water • Strutter • Up Around the Bend.

00702560 Book/CD Pack....... $14.99

2. ACOUSTIC TOP HITS

About a Girl • I'm Yours • The Lazy Song • The Scientist • 21 Guns • Upside Down • What I Got • Wonderwall.

00702569 Book/CD Pack....... $14.99

3. ROCK HITS

All the Small Things • Best of You • Brain Stew (The Godzilla Remix) • Californication • Island in the Sun • Plush • Smells Like Teen Spirit • Use Somebody.

00702570 Book/CD Pack....... $14.99

4. ROCK 'N' ROLL

Blue Suede Shoes • I Get Around • I'm a Believer • Jailhouse Rock • Oh, Pretty Woman • Peggy Sue • Runaway • Wake Up Little Susie.

00702572 Book/CD Pack....... $14.99

6. CHRISTMAS SONGS

Have Yourself a Merry Little Christmas • A Holly Jolly Christmas • The Little Drummer Boy • Run Rudolph Run • Santa Claus Is Comin' to Town • Silver and Gold • Sleigh Ride • Winter Wonderland.

00101879 Book/CD Pack......... $14.99

7. BLUES SONGS FOR BEGINNERS

Come On (Part 1) • Double Trouble • Gangster of Love • I'm Ready • Let Me Love You Baby • Mary Had a Little Lamb • San-Ho-Zay • T-Bone Shuffle.

00103235 Book/CD Pack........ $14.99

8. ACOUSTIC SONGS FOR BEGINNERS

Barely Breathing • Drive • Everlong • Good Riddance (Time of Your Life) • Hallelujah • Hey There Delilah • Lake of Fire • Photograph.

00103240 Book/CD Pack....$14.99

9. ROCK SONGS FOR BEGINNERS

Are You Gonna Be My Girl • Buddy Holly • Everybody Hurts • In Bloom • Otherside • The Rock Show • Santa Monica • When I Come Around.

00103255 Book/CD Pack.....$14.99

10. GREEN DAY

Basket Case • Boulevard of Broken Dreams • Good Riddance (Time of Your Life) • Holiday • Longview • 21 Guns • Wake Me up When September Ends • When I Come Around.

00122322 Book/CD Pack.....$14.99

11. NIRVANA

All Apologies • Come As You Are • Heart Shaped Box • Lake of Fire • Lithium • The Man Who Sold the World • Rape Me • Smells Like Teen Spirit.

00122325 Book/Online Audio........$14.99

12. TAYLOR SWIFT

Fifteen • Love Story • Mean • Picture to Burn • Red • We Are Never Ever Getting Back Together • White Horse • You Belong with Me.

00122326 Book/CD Pack.....$16.99

13. AC/DC

Back in Black • Dirty Deeds Done Dirt Cheap • For Those About to Rock (We Salute You) • Hells Bells • Highway to Hell • Rock and Roll Ain't Noise Pollution • T.N.T. • You Shook Me All Night Long.

14042895 Book/Online Audio........$16.99

14. JIMI HENDRIX – SMASH HITS

All Along the Watchtower • Can You See Me • Crosstown Traffic • Fire • Foxey Lady • Hey Joe • Manic Depression • Purple Haze • Red House • Remember • Stone Free • The Wind Cries Mary.

00130591 Book/Online Audio........$24.99

HAL•LEONARD®

www.halleonard.com

Prices, contents, and availability subject to change without notice.

HAL•LEONARD® GUITAR PLAY-ALONG

AUDIO ACCESS INCLUDED

This series will help you play your favorite songs quickly and easily. Just follow **INCLUDES TAB** the tab and listen to the audio to the hear how the guitar should sound, and then play along using the separate backing tracks. Audio files also include software to slow down the tempo without changing pitch. The melody and lyrics are included in the book so that you can sing or simply follow along.

VOL. 1 – ROCK	00699570 / $16.99	
VOL. 2 – ACOUSTIC	00699569 / $16.99	
VOL. 3 – HARD ROCK	00699573 / $17.99	
VOL. 4 – POP/ROCK	00699571 / $16.99	
VOL. 6 – '90S ROCK	00699572 / $16.99	
VOL. 7 – BLUES	00699575 / $17.99	
VOL. 8 – ROCK	00699585 / $16.99	
VOL. 9 – EASY ACOUSTIC SONGS	00151708 / $16.99	
VOL. 10 – ACOUSTIC	00699586 / $16.95	
VOL. 11 – EARLY ROCK	00699579 / $14.95	
VOL. 12 – POP/ROCK	00699587 / $14.95	
VOL. 13 – FOLK ROCK	00699581 / $15.99	
VOL. 14 – BLUES ROCK	00699582 / $16.99	
VOL. 15 – R&B	00699583 / $16.99	
VOL. 16 – JAZZ	00699584 / $15.95	
VOL. 17 – COUNTRY	00699588 / $16.99	
VOL. 18 – ACOUSTIC ROCK	00699577 / $15.95	
VOL. 19 – SOUL	00699578 / $15.99	
VOL. 20 – ROCKABILLY	00699580 / $14.95	
VOL. 21 – SANTANA	00174525 / $17.99	
VOL. 22 – CHRISTMAS	00699600 / $15.99	
VOL. 23 – SURF	00699635 / $15.99	
VOL. 24 – ERIC CLAPTON	00699649 / $17.99	
VOL. 25 – THE BEATLES	00198265 / $17.99	
VOL. 26 – ELVIS PRESLEY	00699643 / $16.99	
VOL. 27 – DAVID LEE ROTH	00699645 / $16.95	
VOL. 28 – GREG KOCH	00699646 / $16.99	
VOL. 29 – BOB SEGER	00699647 / $15.99	
VOL. 30 – KISS	00699644 / $16.99	
VOL. 31 – CHRISTMAS HITS	00699652 / $14.95	
VOL. 32 – THE OFFSPRING	00699653 / $14.95	
VOL. 33 – ACOUSTIC CLASSICS	00699656 / $17.99	
VOL. 34 – CLASSIC ROCK	00699658 / $17.99	
VOL. 35 – HAIR METAL	00699660 / $17.99	
VOL. 36 – SOUTHERN ROCK	00699661 / $16.95	
VOL. 37 – ACOUSTIC UNPLUGGED	00699662 / $22.99	
VOL. 38 – BLUES	00699663 / $16.95	
VOL. 39 – '80S METAL	00699664 / $16.99	
VOL. 40 – INCUBUS	00699668 / $17.95	
VOL. 41 – ERIC CLAPTON	00699669 / $17.99	
VOL. 42 – COVER BAND HITS	00211597 / $16.99	
VOL. 43 – LYNYRD SKYNYRD	00699681 / $17.95	
VOL. 44 – JAZZ	00699689 / $16.99	
VOL. 45 – TV THEMES	00699718 / $14.95	
VOL. 46 – MAINSTREAM ROCK	00699722 / $16.95	
VOL. 47 – HENDRIX SMASH HITS	00699723 / $19.99	
VOL. 48 – AEROSMITH CLASSICS	00699724 / $17.99	
VOL. 49 – STEVIE RAY VAUGHAN	00699725 / $17.99	
VOL. 50 – VAN HALEN 1978-1984	00110269 / $17.99	
VOL. 51 – ALTERNATIVE '90S	00699727 / $14.99	
VOL. 52 – FUNK	00699728 / $15.99	
VOL. 53 – DISCO	00699729 / $14.99	
VOL. 54 – HEAVY METAL	00699730 / $15.99	
VOL. 55 – POP METAL	00699731 / $14.95	
VOL. 56 – FOO FIGHTERS	00699749 / $15.99	
VOL. 59 – CHET ATKINS	00702347 / $16.99	
VOL. 62 – CHRISTMAS CAROLS	00699798 / $12.95	
VOL. 63 – CREEDENCE CLEARWATER REVIVAL	00699802 / $16.99	
VOL. 64 – THE ULTIMATE OZZY OSBOURNE	00699803 / $17.99	
VOL. 66 – THE ROLLING STONES	00699807 / $17.99	
VOL. 67 – BLACK SABBATH	00699808 / $16.99	

VOL. 68 – PINK FLOYD – DARK SIDE OF THE MOON	00699809 / $16.99	
VOL. 69 – ACOUSTIC FAVORITES	00699810 / $16.99	
VOL. 70 – OZZY OSBOURNE	00699805 / $16.99	
VOL. 71 – CHRISTIAN ROCK	00699824 / $14.95	
VOL. 73 – BLUESY ROCK	00699829 / $16.99	
VOL. 74 – SIMPLE STRUMMING SONGS	00151706 / $19.99	
VOL. 75 – TOM PETTY	00699882 / $16.99	
VOL. 76 – COUNTRY HITS	00699884 / $14.95	
VOL. 77 – BLUEGRASS	00699910 / $15.99	
VOL. 78 – NIRVANA	00700132 / $16.99	
VOL. 79 – NEIL YOUNG	00700133 / $24.99	
VOL. 80 – ACOUSTIC ANTHOLOGY	00700175 / $19.95	
VOL. 81 – ROCK ANTHOLOGY	00700176 / $22.99	
VOL. 82 – EASY SONGS	00700177 / $14.99	
VOL. 83 – THREE CHORD SONGS	00700178 / $16.99	
VOL. 84 – STEELY DAN	00700200 / $16.99	
VOL. 85 – THE POLICE	00700269 / $16.99	
VOL. 86 – BOSTON	00700465 / $16.99	
VOL. 87 – ACOUSTIC WOMEN	00700763 / $14.99	
VOL. 89 – REGGAE	00700468 / $15.99	
VOL. 90 – CLASSICAL POP	00700469 / $14.99	
VOL. 91 – BLUES INSTRUMENTALS	00700505 / $15.99	
VOL. 92 – EARLY ROCK INSTRUMENTALS	00700506 / $15.99	
VOL. 93 – ROCK INSTRUMENTALS	00700507 / $16.99	
VOL. 94 – SLOW BLUES	00700508 / $16.99	
VOL. 95 – BLUES CLASSICS	00700509 / $14.99	
VOL. 99 – ZZ TOP	00700762 / $16.99	
VOL. 100 – B.B. KING	00700466 / $16.99	
VOL. 101 – SONGS FOR BEGINNERS	00701917 / $14.99	
VOL. 102 – CLASSIC PUNK	00700769 / $14.99	
VOL. 103 – SWITCHFOOT	00700773 / $16.99	
VOL. 104 – DUANE ALLMAN	00700846 / $16.99	
VOL. 105 – LATIN	00700939 / $16.99	
VOL. 106 – WEEZER	00700958 / $14.99	
VOL. 107 – CREAM	00701069 / $16.99	
VOL. 108 – THE WHO	00701053 / $16.99	
VOL. 109 – STEVE MILLER	00701054 / $16.99	
VOL. 110 – SLIDE GUITAR HITS	00701055 / $16.99	
VOL. 111 – JOHN MELLENCAMP	00701056 / $14.99	
VOL. 112 – QUEEN	00701052 / $16.99	
VOL. 113 – JIM CROCE	00701058 / $15.99	
VOL. 114 – BON JOVI	00701060 / $16.99	
VOL. 115 – JOHNNY CASH	00701070 / $16.99	
VOL. 116 – THE VENTURES	00701124 / $16.99	
VOL. 117 – BRAD PAISLEY	00701224 / $16.99	
VOL. 118 – ERIC JOHNSON	00701353 / $16.99	
VOL. 119 – AC/DC CLASSICS	00701356 / $17.99	
VOL. 120 – PROGRESSIVE ROCK	00701457 / $14.99	
VOL. 121 – U2	00701508 / $16.99	
VOL. 122 – CROSBY, STILLS & NASH	00701610 / $16.99	
VOL. 123 – LENNON & MCCARTNEY ACOUSTIC	00701614 / $16.99	
VOL. 125 – JEFF BECK	00701687 / $16.99	
VOL. 126 – BOB MARLEY	00701701 / $16.99	
VOL. 127 – 1970S ROCK	00701739 / $16.99	
VOL. 128 – 1960S ROCK	00701740 / $14.99	
VOL. 129 – MEGADETH	00701741 / $16.99	
VOL. 130 – IRON MAIDEN	00701742 / $17.99	
VOL. 131 – 1990S ROCK	00701743 / $14.99	
VOL. 132 – COUNTRY ROCK	00701757 / $15.99	
VOL. 133 – TAYLOR SWIFT	00701894 / $16.99	
VOL. 134 – AVENGED SEVENFOLD	00701906 / $16.99	
VOL. 135 – MINOR BLUES	00151350 / $17.99	

VOL. 136 – GUITAR THEMES	00701922 / $14.99	
VOL. 137 – IRISH TUNES	00701966 / $15.99	
VOL. 138 – BLUEGRASS CLASSICS	00701967 / $14.99	
VOL. 139 – GARY MOORE	00702370 / $16.99	
VOL. 140 – MORE STEVIE RAY VAUGHAN	00702396 / $17.99	
VOL. 141 – ACOUSTIC HITS	00702401 / $16.99	
VOL. 143 – SLASH	00702425 / $19.99	
VOL. 144 – DJANGO REINHARDT	00702531 / $16.99	
VOL. 145 – DEF LEPPARD	00702532 / $17.99	
VOL. 146 – ROBERT JOHNSON	00702533 / $16.99	
VOL. 147 – SIMON & GARFUNKEL	14041591 / $16.99	
VOL. 148 – BOB DYLAN	14041592 / $16.99	
VOL. 149 – AC/DC HITS	14041593 / $17.99	
VOL. 150 – ZAKK WYLDE	02501717 / $16.99	
VOL. 151 – J.S. BACH	02501730 / $16.99	
VOL. 152 – JOE BONAMASSA	02501751 / $19.99	
VOL. 153 – RED HOT CHILI PEPPERS	00702990 / $19.99	
VOL. 155 – ERIC CLAPTON – FROM THE ALBUM UNPLUGGED	00703085 / $16.99	
VOL. 156 – SLAYER	00703770 / $17.99	
VOL. 157 – FLEETWOOD MAC	00101382 / $16.99	
VOL. 158 – ULTIMATE CHRISTMAS	00101889 / $14.99	
VOL. 159 – WES MONTGOMERY	00102593 / $19.99	
VOL. 160 – T-BONE WALKER	00102641 / $16.99	
VOL. 161 – THE EAGLES – ACOUSTIC	00102659 / $17.99	
VOL. 162 – THE EAGLES HITS	00102667 / $17.99	
VOL. 163 – PANTERA	00103036 / $17.99	
VOL. 164 – VAN HALEN 1986-1995	00110270 / $17.99	
VOL. 165 – GREEN DAY	00210343 / $17.99	
VOL. 166 – MODERN BLUES	00700764 / $16.99	
VOL. 167 – DREAM THEATER	00111938 / $24.99	
VOL. 168 – KISS	00113421 / $16.99	
VOL. 169 – TAYLOR SWIFT	00115982 / $16.99	
VOL. 170 – THREE DAYS GRACE	00117337 / $16.99	
VOL. 171 – JAMES BROWN	00117420 / $16.99	
VOL. 172 – THE DOOBIE BROTHERS	00119670 / $16.99	
VOL. 174 – SCORPIONS	00122119 / $16.99	
VOL. 175 – MICHAEL SCHENKER	00122127 / $16.99	
VOL. 176 – BLUES BREAKERS WITH JOHN MAYALL & ERIC CLAPTON	00122132 / $19.99	
VOL. 177 – ALBERT KING	00123271 / $16.99	
VOL. 178 – JASON MRAZ	00124165 / $17.99	
VOL. 179 – RAMONES	00127073 / $16.99	
VOL. 180 – BRUNO MARS	00129706 / $16.99	
VOL. 181 – JACK JOHNSON	00129854 / $16.99	
VOL. 182 – SOUNDGARDEN	00138161 / $17.99	
VOL. 183 – BUDDY GUY	00138240 / $17.99	
VOL. 184 – KENNY WAYNE SHEPHERD	00138258 / $17.99	
VOL. 185 – JOE SATRIANI	00139457 / $17.99	
VOL. 186 – GRATEFUL DEAD	00139459 / $17.99	
VOL. 187 – JOHN DENVER	00140839 / $17.99	
VOL. 188 – MÖTLEY CRUE	00141145 / $17.99	
VOL. 189 – JOHN MAYER	00144350 / $17.99	
VOL. 191 – PINK FLOYD CLASSICS	00146164 / $17.99	
VOL. 192 – JUDAS PRIEST	00151352 / $17.99	

Prices, contents, and availability subject to change without notice.

Complete song lists available online.

www.halleonard.com

0817